THE

EVERY KIDS'

Halloween Puzzle & Activity Book

Hours of spine-tingling fun!

Beth L. Blair & Jennifer A. Ericsson

Adams Media Corporation
Avon, Massachusetts

EDITORIAL
Publishing Director: Gary M. Krebs
Managing Editor: Kate McBride
Copy Chief: Laura MacLaughlin
Acquisitions Editor: Bethany Brown
Development Editor: Julie Gutin
Production Editor: Khrysti Nazzaro

PRODUCTION
Production Director: Susan Beale
Production Manager: Michelle Roy Kelly
Series Designer: Colleen Cunningham
Layout and Graphics: Paul Beatrice,
Colleen Cunningham, Rachael Eiben,
Daria Perreault, Erin Ring, Frank Rivera

An *Everything*® Series Book.
Everything® and everything.com® are registered trademarks of F+W Publications, Inc.

Published by Adams Media, an F+W Publications Company
57 Littlefield Street, Avon, MA 02322 U.S.A.
www.adamsmedia.com

ISBN: 1-58062-959-8

Printed in the United States of America.

J   I   H   G   F   E   D

Cover illustrations by Dana Regan.
Interior illustrations by Kurt Dolber.
Puzzles by Beth Blair.

Puzzle Power Software by Centron Software Technologies, Inc. was used to create puzzle grids.

This book is available at quantity discounts for bulk purchases.
For information, call 1-800-872-5627.

See the entire Everything® series at *www.everything.com*.

CONTENTS

Introduction

If you're like us, Halloween is one of your favorite holidays. After all, how many times do you get to dress up in fun costumes, roam the neighborhood after dark, and come home with a bag loaded with goodies? Only once a year!

We've created *The Everything® Kids' Halloween Puzzle & Activity Book* to help keep you in the Halloween mood long after the day itself is over. And because we know that not everyone likes the same kinds of puzzles, we've included a variety from which you can choose. There are mazes, word searches, codes, picture puzzles, math puzzles—and much more! Not only will you have fun trying to solve them all, but you just might learn a little something new about Halloween along the way.

For instance, in ancient Ireland when peasants visited house after house, they were *not* hoping to get candy. **Can you find five items in this word search that they might have wanted?**

L N R O M A G E
P R E T A C O G
P O T A T O E S
A C T P H I G E
B O U R U N G L
E R B E E S S A

So whether you're into pumpkins or parties, haunted houses or scary monsters, we've got plenty of puzzles for you to try. We hope you have a howling good time!

Beth L. Blair   *Jennifer A. Ericsson*

Tasty Pastry

Candy was not the original Halloween treat. At first, homeowners gave a certain kind of pastry. It was supposed to keep them safe from pranks and help them get into heaven after they died.

Start with one of the "**S**"s in the grid. Move right, left, up, or down ONLY. When you have chosen the correct path, you will have spelled out the two-word answer.

HINT: Use the rebus clue to help sound out the words to look for!

Seeing the Future

In the past, some Halloween games were supposed to help predict the future. Girls would peel the skin from an apple in one long piece. Then they would swing the peel around three times and throw it over their shoulder. What would they learn from this?

To find out, start at the **T marked with a dot**. Collect every other letter until you reach the center. Then start at the very beginning again and collect all the letters you missed the first time!

HINT: Write the letters in the space below, and cross them out as you go around the peel.

Why a Disguise?

Hundreds of years ago, people wore masks and disguises on Halloween night, like we do today. Why did they do this? Answer as many clues below as you can, and fill the letters you have into the grid. Work back and forth between the box and clues until you can read the reason why people dressed up in the past. **HINT:** One word has been done for you.

1K	2G	3D	4K		5H	6D	7I	8E	9C		10C	11B	
12J	13K	14I	15I	16F		17A **K**	18F	19G	20E		21A **E**	22D	23A **I**	24E
25B	26H	27F	28D	29J	30A **T**	31G		32B	33F	34H	35I		
36B	37H	38G	39C		40J	41E	42C	43I					

A. Toy that is flown at the end of a long string.

$$\frac{K}{17} \ \frac{I}{23} \ \frac{T}{30} \ \frac{E}{21}$$

B. Opposite of slow.

$$\overline{36} \ \overline{32} \ \overline{25} \ \overline{11}$$

C. Ten cents.

$$\overline{9} \ \overline{10} \ \overline{39} \ \overline{42}$$

D. Opposite of under.

$$\overline{6} \ \overline{22} \ \overline{3} \ \overline{28}$$

E. Give someone a hand.

$$\overline{41} \ \overline{8} \ \overline{24} \ \overline{20}$$

F. Opposite of narrow.

$$\overline{33} \ \overline{27} \ \overline{16} \ \overline{18}$$

G. What you wear on a foot.

$$\overline{31} \ \overline{2} \ \overline{38} \ \overline{19}$$

H. Musical instrument with strings.

$$\overline{5} \ \overline{34} \ \overline{37} \ \overline{26}$$

I. Mashed potatoes should not be this way.

$$\overline{15} \ \overline{14} \ \overline{43} \ \overline{7} \ \overline{35}$$

J. Ability to make clever jokes.

$$\overline{12} \ \overline{29} \ \overline{40}$$

K. Something to play with.

$$\overline{1} \ \overline{13} \ \overline{4}$$

What food is traditionally served on October 31?

Halloweeners!

🕷 🕷 🕷 🕷 **3** 🕷 🕷 🕷 🕷

Orange and Black

What two colors do you automatically think of when someone says *Halloween*? Orange and black, of course! Answer the clues below with the names of orange things and black things. Then unscramble the circled letters to find two words that describe why these colors represent Halloween.

Orange fruits for carving.

_ _ _ _ _ _O_ _O_

A golden summer flower.

_ _ _ _ _O_ _ _

Gather ripe crops.

O_ _ _ _ _ _ _O_

They turn orange in autumn.

O_ _ _ _ _O_

Flickering tongues of fire.

_ _ _ _ _O_ _

A bright light in the sky at night.

_ _ _O_

You write on it with chalk.

_ _ _ _ O_ _ _ _ _ _

Furry pets that catch mice.

_ _ _ O_

Sidewalk or street covering.

_O_ _ _ _O_ _ _

Opposite of day.

O_ _ _ _

Opposite of life.

O_ _ _ _

A web-spinner.

O_ _ _ _ _O_

What does "orange" represent?	What does "black" represent?

You Look Familiar

According to legend, witches had one or more pet animals called "familiars." It was believed that the witch could take the shape of this animal whenever she pleased.

Color all the triangles in this picture and you will see a familiar familiar!

Celtic Celebration

Cross out every word that names a holiday in some part of the world. When you are finished, collect the leftover letters from left to right, and top to bottom. Write them, in order, in the blanks to discover the name of the ancient Celtic festival from which Halloween evolved.

HINT: The answer looks *nothing* like the word Halloween!

```
C H R I S T M A S
S F A S S I K A A
P U R I M H O L I
M C A R N I V A L
K W A N Z A A H A
I N N E W Y E A R
```

Holidays to be crossed out:
Carnival
Christmas
Fassika
Holi
Kwanzaa
New Year
Purim

How Symbolic

Do you ever see jack-o-lanterns at Christmas, or witches on the 4th of July? No way! Over the years, certain symbols have come to especially represent Halloween. Find these three groups of symbols in the grid.

Group 1

Group 2

Group 3

Superstitious Words

A superstition is a belief based on ignorance and fear. People in the past were very superstitious about Halloween, and often used magic words to protect themselves from the scary things they did not understand. How many words can you create from the word **S-U-P-E-R-S-T-I-T-I-O-N?** Bet you can make at least fifty!

SUPERSTITION

1. _____
2. _____
3. _____
4. _____
5. _____
6. _____
7. _____
8. _____
9. _____
10. _____
11. _____
12. _____
13. _____
14. _____
15. _____
16. _____
17. _____

18. _____
19. _____
20. _____
21. _____
22. _____
23. _____
24. _____
25. _____
26. _____
27. _____
28. _____
29. _____
30. _____
31. _____
32. _____
33. _____
34. _____

35. _____
36. _____
37. _____
38. _____
39. _____
40. _____
41. _____
42. _____
43. _____
44. _____
45. _____
46. _____
47. _____
48. _____
49. _____
50. _____

Day of the Dead

People in Mexico don't celebrate Halloween, but they do celebrate "Day of the Dead." This happy festival is for remembering family and friends who have died. People visit the cemetery, have special dinners, dance, and eat candy.

Five words that mean the same thing as the word "dead" are hidden in this grid. To find them, take one letter from each column moving from left to right. Each letter can only be used once, so cross them off as you use them. The first word is done for you.

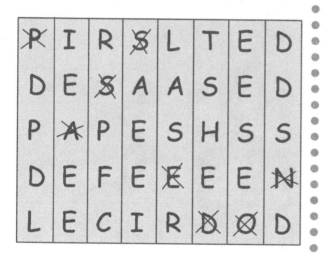

1. <u> PASSED   ON </u>

2. _____

3. _____

4. _____

5. _____

Bread of the Dead

Some Mexican families celebrate Day of the Dead with a special "Bread of the Dead" (*pan de muerto*). It is considered good luck if you bite into a certain toy that is hidden within each loaf. Color the boxes marked with a dot in the *upper right* corner to see what the toy is.

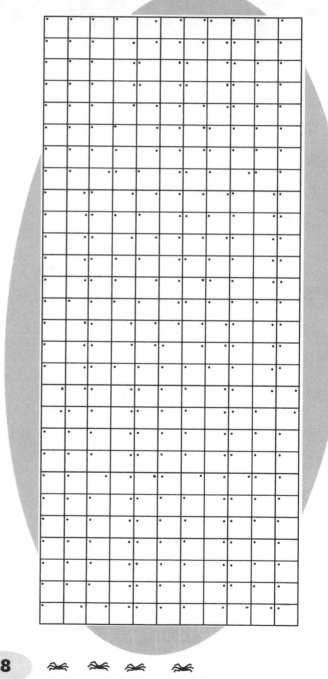

Double Trouble

People used to believe that witches spent a lot of time stirring brews in their cauldrons and chanting spells. Break the code to hear what these witches are saying.

Start with a simple number substitution code (A=1, B=2, C=3, etc). But wait! Since there are **TWO** witches, all the numbers are doubled!

8 – 30 – 42 – 4 – 24 – 10,

8 – 30 – 42 – 4 – 24 – 10,

40 – 30 – 18 – 24

2 – 28 – 8

40 – 36 – 30 – 42 – 4 – 24 – 10

12 – 18 – 36 – 10

4 – 42 – 36 – 28,

2 – 28 – 8

6 – 2 – 42 – 24 – 8 – 36 – 30 – 28

4 – 42 – 4 – 4 – 24 – 10

American colonists were terrified of witches. One place in New England is particularly famous for the number of witch hunts and trials that occurred there. Use the same code to find out where this city is.

38 – 2 – 24 – 10 – 26,

26 – 2 – 38 – 38.

Creepy Carving

A certain carving used to be put on gravestones to protect the soul of the person buried underneath it, and to prevent the soul from returning as a ghost. To see what that carving looked like, use a pencil to follow the dots in numerical order. Center a penny on each X and trace around them to complete the drawing.

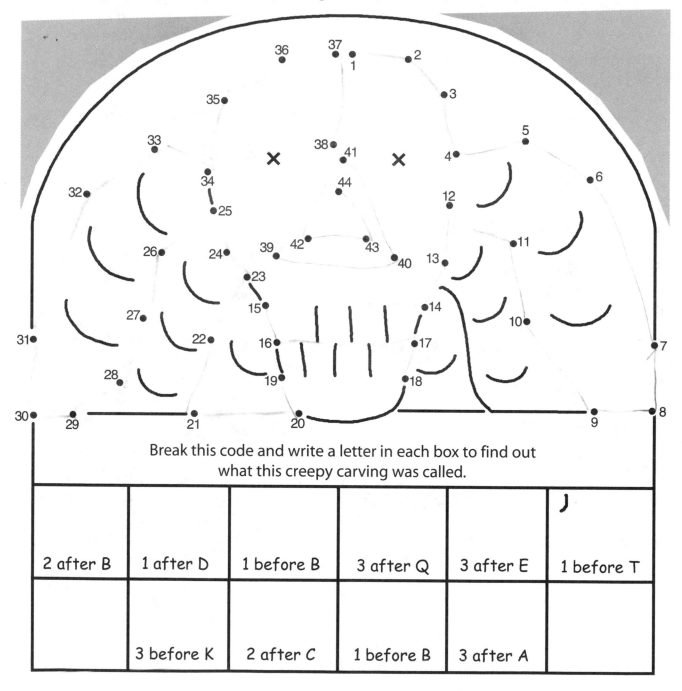

Break this code and write a letter in each box to find out what this creepy carving was called.

					ʃ
2 after B	1 after D	1 before B	3 after Q	3 after E	1 before T
	3 before K	2 after C	1 before B	3 after A	

Hello Again

A very famous magician and escape artist died in 1926 on Halloween night. He claimed that if there were truly a way to contact the living after one's death, he would do so. People are still waiting to hear from him!

There are twelve magician's props listed below. Write each one in its proper row *across* the grid. When you're finished, read *down* the shaded blocks to learn the famous magician's name.

HINT: We left you a **S-E-A-N-C-E** (a meeting to communicate with spirits) to help you out.

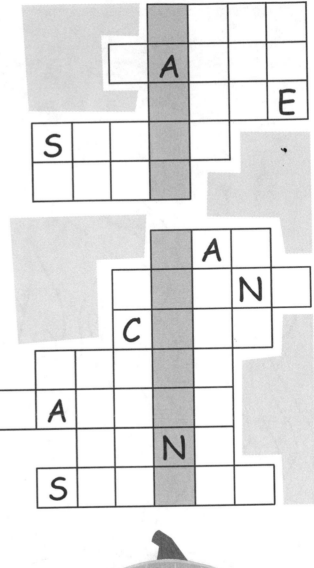

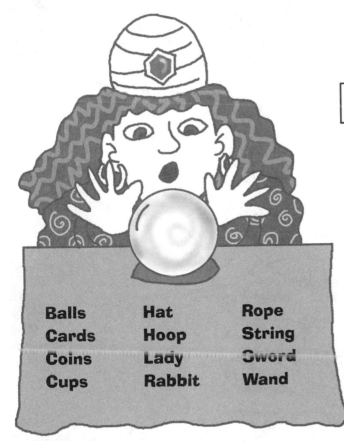

Balls	Hat	Rope
Cards	Hoop	String
Coins	Lady	Sword
Cups	Rabbit	Wand

Why did the ghost refuse to talk to the spiritualist?

Because she called collect!

Burning Bonfire

Bonfires were often used to scare evil spirits away. Find your way from **START** to **END**, through the burning flames, to banish this evil spirit.

END

START

Chapter 2
The Pumpkin Patch

Yummy Pumpkins

Take the letters in each pumpkin, add one missing letter, and unscramble them to discover the name of six delicious foods made from pumpkins. The missing letters read from top to bottom to spell out the name of another part of the pumpkin that is good to eat.

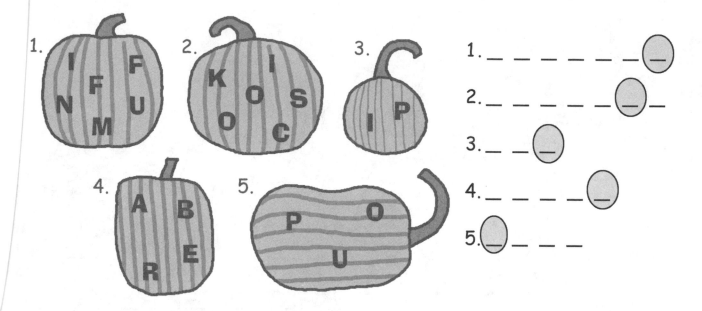

1. _ _ _ _ _ _ (_)

2. _ _ _ _ (_) _

3. _ _ (_)

4. _ _ _ _ (_)

5. (_) _ _ _

Smashed Pumpkins

Oops! Some Halloween trickster has smashed this jack-o-lantern.
Which one of the four faces do you get when you put the pieces together again?

Carve-a-thon

Jack-o-lanterns have many different expressions on their faces. Unscramble the words at the bottom of the page, and match each to a jack-o-lantern.

1. D A S _____

2. D S P R S U R I E _____

3. N I K I W N G _____

4. Y F O O G _____

5. R A S C Y _____

6. Y O T O T H _____

Pumpkin Patch

Sarah has lost her perfect pumpkin. Can you find the pumpkin that matches the one on Sarah's poster?

Smile!

Shade in the numbered boxes that are listed for each row. Be sure to fill in each box carefully, and keep track of which row you're on!

SPECIAL DIRECTIONS: If there is a set of numbers with a dash between them (for example 5-16), that means you must shade in box 5, box 16, AND all the numbers in between!

What do you use to fix a broken pumpkin?

A pumpkin patch!

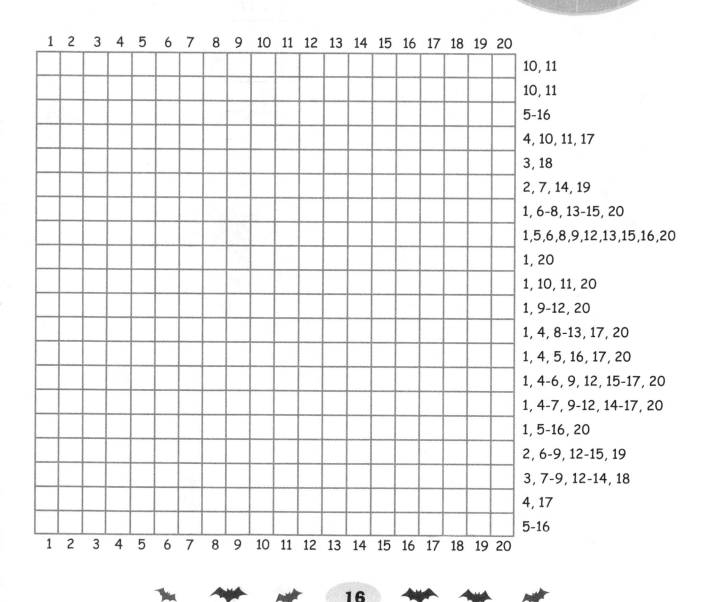

Row	Numbers to shade
1	10, 11
2	10, 11
3	5-16
4	4, 10, 11, 17
5	3, 18
6	2, 7, 14, 19
7	1, 6-8, 13-15, 20
8	1,5,6,8,9,12,13,15,16,20
9	1, 20
10	1, 10, 11, 20
11	1, 9-12, 20
12	1, 4, 8-13, 17, 20
13	1, 4, 5, 16, 17, 20
14	1, 4-6, 9, 12, 15-17, 20
15	1, 4-7, 9-12, 14-17, 20
16	1, 5-16, 20
17	2, 6-9, 12-15, 19
18	3, 7-9, 12-14, 18
19	4, 17
20	5-16

How Big?

Every year, gardeners all over the world try to grow the biggest pumpkin. When you have filled in the grid correctly, you will know something about the prizewinners. The letters in each column go in the squares directly below them, but maybe not in the same order! Black squares are the spaces between words.

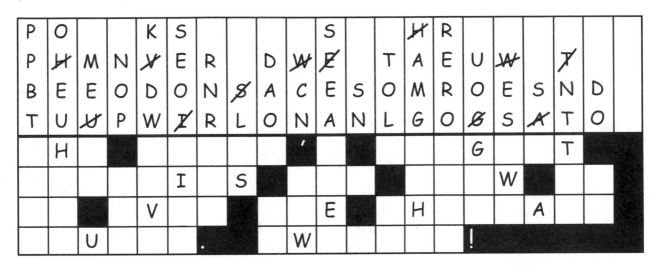

Sad Jack / Glad Jack

Some jack-o-lanterns have happy faces. Some jack-o-lanterns do not. Can you help Sad Jack move through the maze so that he has a happy face at the end? Make a path that alternates Sad Jack and Glad Jack. You can move up and down, or side to side, but not diagonally. If you hit a Mad Jack, you are going in the wrong direction!

START

END

Squiggle Giggles

What kind of faces do you like on your jack-o-lanterns? Use the lines on the pumpkins below to help you make a whole pile of funny faces.

Wacky Word

_ _ _ _ _ _ _ _: a fat, orange fruit that sits on the doorstep at Halloween.

To find the wacky word, color in the letters **F-A-T** in the grid below. Read the remaining letters.

F A P F L A A
U F M P A K
T I A F N A A

Missing Pumpkin

The words below are missing the letters **P-U-M-P-K-I-N.** Use the clues provided to figure them out.

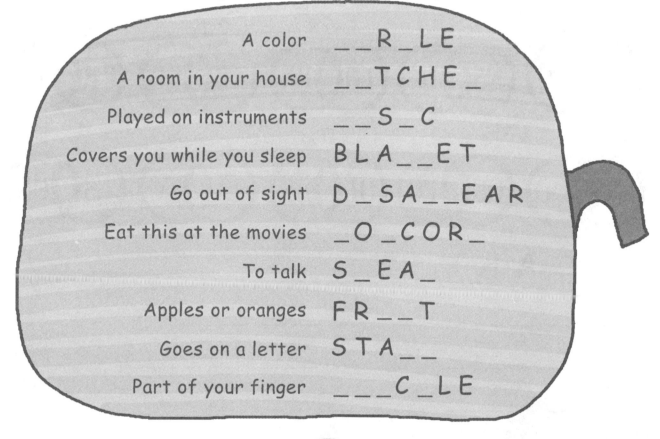

Clue	Answer
A color	_ _ R _ L E
A room in your house	_ _ T C H E _
Played on instruments	_ _ S _ C
Covers you while you sleep	B L A _ _ E T
Go out of sight	D _ S A _ _ E A R
Eat this at the movies	_ O _ C O R _
To talk	S _ E A _
Apples or oranges	F R _ _ T
Goes on a letter	S T A _ _
Part of your finger	_ _ _ C _ L E

Pumpkin Rings

Pumpkins were not the original jack-o-lanterns. Solve this puzzle to find out which vegetables were carved with faces before the pumpkin. Look carefully at these rings. Some look like they are linked through each other. Others look like two rings that overlap, but are NOT linked. In the blanks provided underneath, copy down, in order, only the letters you find inside the unlinked rings. The first few have been done for you.

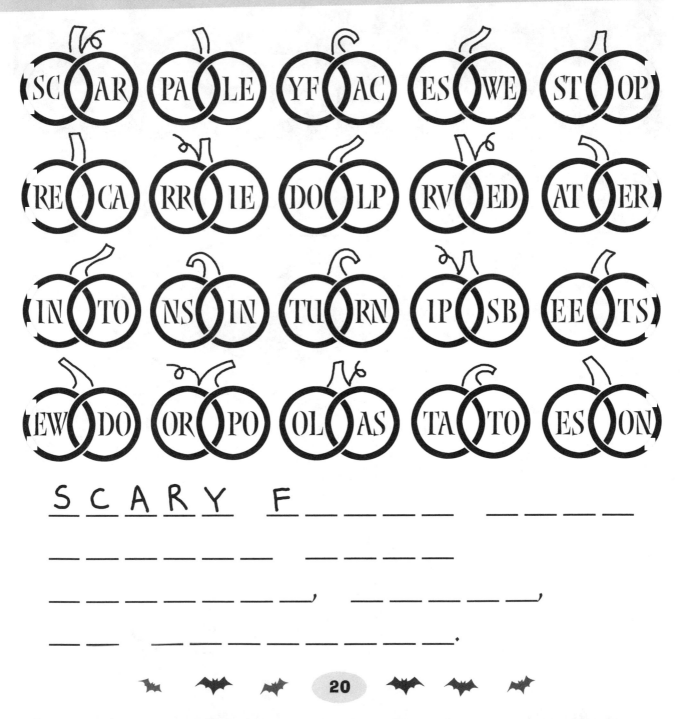

S C A R Y F _ _ _ _ _ _ _ _

_ _ _ _ _ _ _ _ _ _

_ _ _ _ _ _ _ _ , _ _ _ _ _ ,

_ _ _ _ _ _ _ _ _ _ .

Pounds of Pumpkins

This pumpkin patch has more than 100 pounds of pumpkins in it. Place + and – signs between the pumpkins in each row so that each equation works.

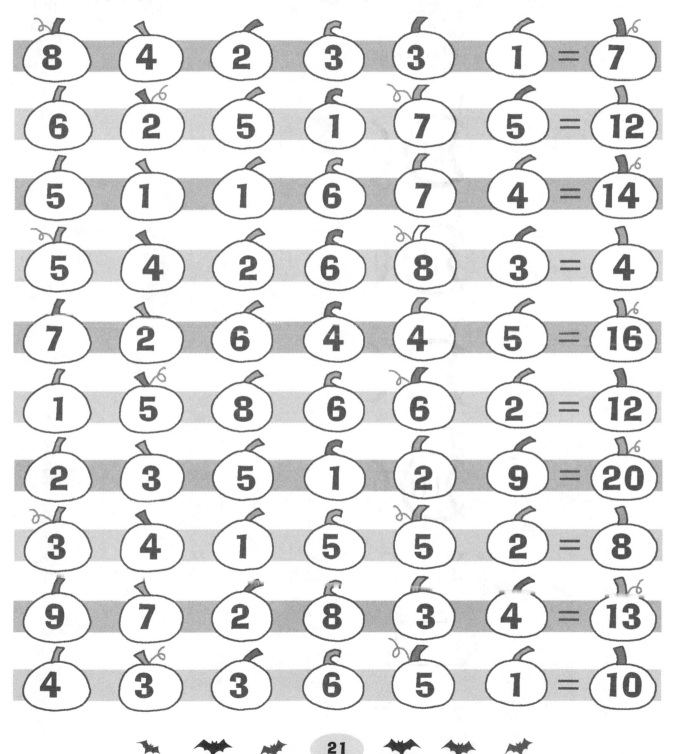

8   4   2   3   3   1 = 7

6   2   5   1   7   5 = 12

5   1   1   6   7   4 = 14

5   4   2   6   8   3 = 4

7   2   6   4   4   5 = 16

1   5   8   6   6   2 = 12

2   3   5   1   2   9 = 20

3   4   1   5   5   2 = 8

9   7   2   8   3   4 = 13

4   3   3   6   5   1 = 10

Perfect Pumpkin

All these words start with a "P," just like "pumpkin." Now, fit them all perfectly into the grid!

Paddle
Pajamas
Papoose
Parsley
Passage
Pat
Patience

Pause
Peddle
Peel
Peep
Pep
Peppermint
Perfume

Pest
Pie
Piece
Pint
Pioneer
Plaster
Pleasant

Poodle
Pop
Possible
Pot
Pound
Present
President

Pressure
Pretzel
Professor
Proud
Provide
Puddle
Pun

HINT: We've left you some P-U-M-P-K-I-N S-E-E-D-S to get you started.

HINT 2: Cross words out of the word list as you use them.

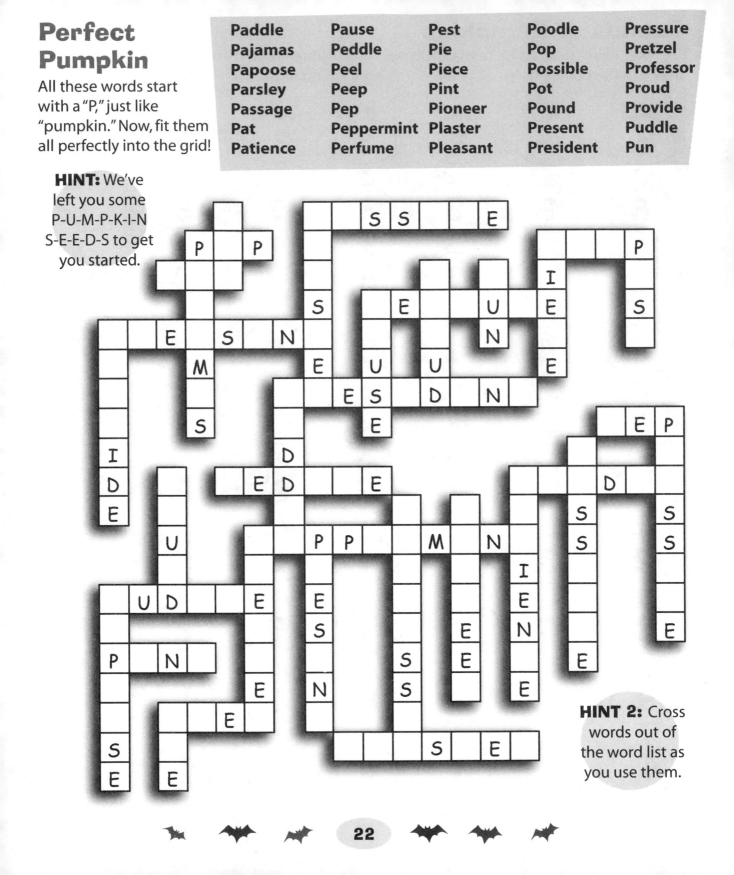

22

Copy Cat

Tim and Kim used identical pumpkins to create two scarecrows. However, they didn't want their creations to be exactly the same. Can you find the thirteen differences? When you're finished, color the scarecrows.

Rebus Riddle

What kind of pumpkin works at the beach?

A   L++F   G+   +D

Piece of Pie

Pumpkin pie is especially good with a swirl of whipped cream on top.
Can you eat your way through this piece of pie from START to END?

START

END

Creepy Crisscross

Have a haunting good time unscrambling these thirteen creepy sounds and fitting them into the crisscross grid. We left you some **B-O-O-S** to get you started.

KEE _____
OBO _____
OLHW _____
OTOH _____
UHDT _____
AONM _____
NLAKC _____
ORAGN _____
WOLRG _____
CLAKCE _____
ARCESM _____
QELUSA _____
LTRAET _____

Spider Speak

Look carefully to figure out the code and answer this riddle:

What is the proper way to greet a ghost?

Haunted Hink Pinks

The answers to Hink Pinks are two rhyming words that each have one syllable. The **BONUS** Hink Pink answer has two words of two syllables!

What does a spook have for breakfast?

___ ___ ___ ___ ___   ___ ___ ___ ___ ___

What did the witch use to clean the cemetery?

___ ___ ___ ___ ___   ___ ___ ___ ___ ___

What is a fast prank?

___ ___ ___ ___ ___   ___ ___ ___ ___ ___

What is a wealthy woman who casts spells?

___ ___ ___ ___   ___ ___ ___ ___ ___

What is a scary evening?

___ ___ ___ ___ ___   ___ ___ ___ ___

What is a really good bunch of magic words?

___ ___ ___ ___ ___   ___ ___ ___ ___ ___

What is a small, really thin, furry animal that flies?

___ ___ ___ ___   ___ ___ ___

BONUS: What is a fun Halloween gathering for kids all dressed as Albert Einstein?

___ ___ ___ ___ ___ ___ ___   ___ ___ ___ ___ ___ ___ ___

Ghostly Message

Color in all the **G**'s and **T**'s and read the remaining letters to find out the answer to this riddle:

What is a ghost's favorite game at a Halloween Party?

Any Body Home?

See if you can find your way from start to end through this totally haunted house. Try not to run into any of the spooky inhabitants!

START

Eek: What happens when a ghost stubs his toe?

Meek: He gets a boo-boo!

THE END

Time for Tea

How many crazy things can you find in this haunted room? There are at least twenty!

Haunted Words

How many words can you find hiding in the word **H-A-U-N-T-E-D**? Bet you can find at least twenty-four!

BONUS: Give yourself a big SHRIEK if you can find any words that are five letters long.

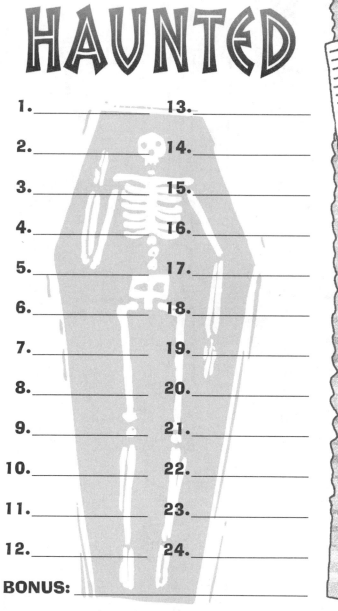

HAUNTED

1._____   13._____

2._____   14._____

3._____   15._____

4._____   16._____

5._____   17._____

6._____   18._____

7._____   19._____

8._____   20._____

9._____   21._____

10._____   22._____

11._____   23._____

12._____   24._____

BONUS: _____

Which Window?

Read the names of six Halloween creatures hidden in the windows of this house. Having trouble? Try finding their names hidden in the word grid at the bottom of the page. Careful—there might be extras!

```
M U M M Y W N R G
K K K S J U A H W
V L X M N T O E W
D A W I Z S R S I
W S M O T E U W T
I Z Z P W L A A C
H Z C O I B Z Z H
I A L L V R A E T
T F T V H X E T F
```

Going Batty

Find the eight bats hidden in this attic.

Just Like a Vampire

Figure out where to put each of the scrambled letters. They all fit under their own columns. When you have filled in the grid correctly, you will have the answer to this riddle:

Why was the vampire kicked out of the haunted house?

B	E	I	N	U	S	N		H	E	P	S	N	S	O	A
P	A	C	A	F	T	E		T	H	E	W	A	E	C	K
	E											S			
	I							H							K

Spider's Choice

Read the web from the center outward to see what spiders like to eat with their hamburgers.

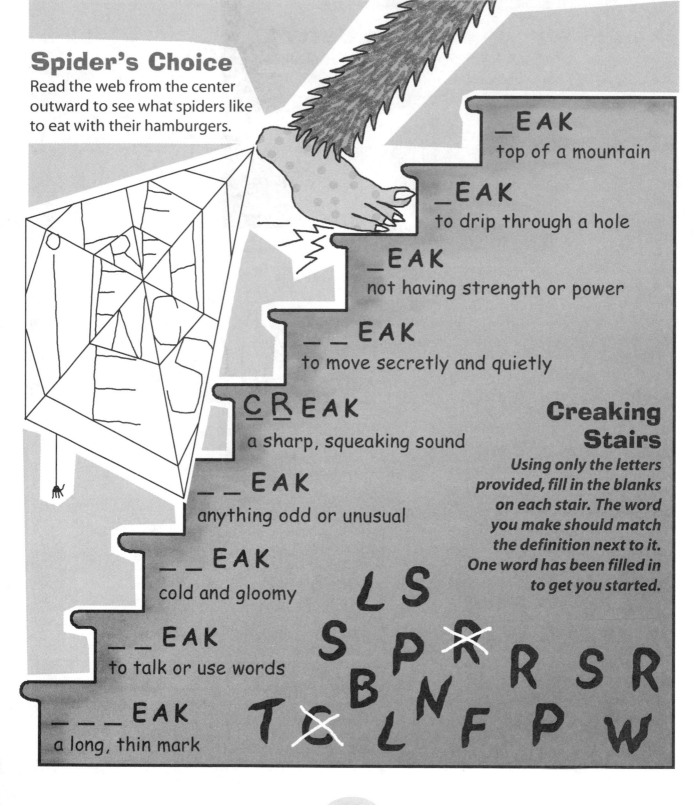

_EAK
top of a mountain

_EAK
to drip through a hole

_EAK
not having strength or power

_ _ EAK
to move secretly and quietly

C R E A K
a sharp, squeaking sound

_ _ EAK
anything odd or unusual

_ _ EAK
cold and gloomy

_ _ EAK
to talk or use words

_ _ _ EAK
a long, thin mark

Creaking Stairs

Using only the letters provided, fill in the blanks on each stair. The word you make should match the definition next to it. One word has been filled in to get you started.

L S
S P R R S R
B N
T C L N F P W

Giggly Gravestones

Spooks have taken names and initials off all the headstones (except one)! Fill in the missing spaces using the names scattered on the ground.

HINT: When you have done it correctly, you should get a laugh from the names in this silly cemetery!

MANNY BONES

YULE B.

DEEP

B.

M.

LEE

GOWIN

B.

SPOOK

ROTT

BACKSOON

IMA

RICK

AL

AMORTIS

DIANE

NING

BARRY

NEXT

IMUS

Boo Who?

These haunted rooms are full of ghosts. Which two ghosts do *not* appear in both rooms?

Two ghosts are telling each other a joke, but they are speaking in "spooktalk." Can you figure out their secret language so you can share the riddle, too?

WBOOHBOOABOOTBOO   IBOOSBOO   ABOO
GBOOHBOOOBOOSBOOTBOO'SBOO
FBOOABOOVBOOOBOORBOOIBOOTBOOEBOO
SBOOONBOOABOOCBOOKBOO
FBOOOBOOOBOOODBOO?

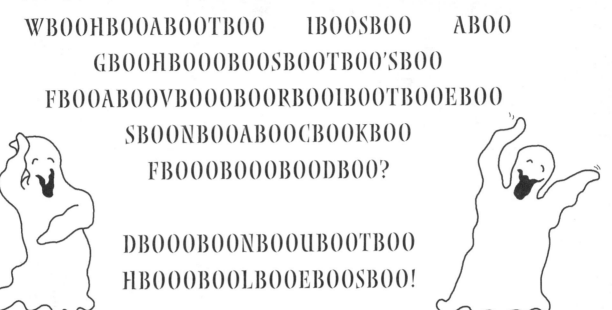

DBOOOBOONBOOUBOOTBOO
HBOOOBOOLBOOEBOOSBOO!

Who's Haunting the House?

Hold this page about a foot away from your eyes, and stare very hard at the black face while counting slowly to thirty. Try not to blink! Then, look at the empty windows or the door of the haunted house. What do you see?

It's a Spooky Day in the Neighborhood

Annie, Drew, Josh, and a ghost all live in the same neighborhood. Using the clues, can you figure out where each child lives, and which house is haunted by the ghost?

- **Annie lives on Pine Street.**
- **A ghost lives diagonally across the street from Josh.**
- **Drew lives down the street from Annie, but on the opposite side.**
- **Josh lives across the street from Annie.**
- **Drew and the ghost live in the same block, but not on the same street.**
- **Josh does not live on Pine Street.**
- **Annie must cross Pine Street to visit Josh or be spooked by the ghost.**

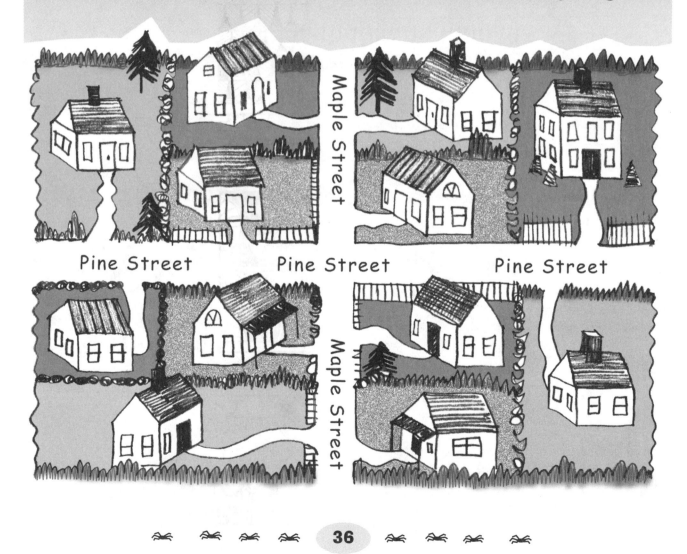

The Big Picture

See what monster is lurking in your neighborhood by following these directions:

1. **Find box 1-A and copy it into square 1-A in the grid.**

2. **Find box 1-B and copy it into square 1-B in the grid.**

3. **Continue doing this until you have copied all the boxes into the grid.**

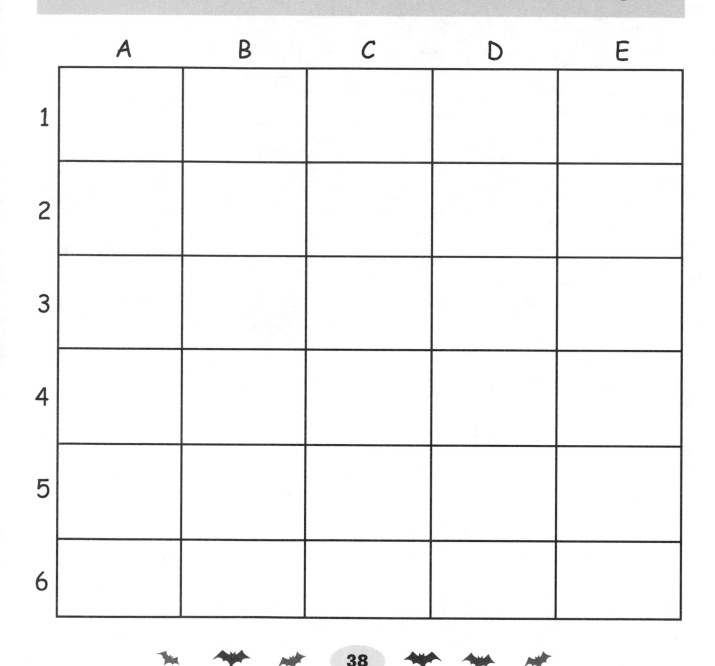

What's the spookiest lake in the USA?

Lake Eerie!

What do little vampires put in their toys?

Bat-teries!

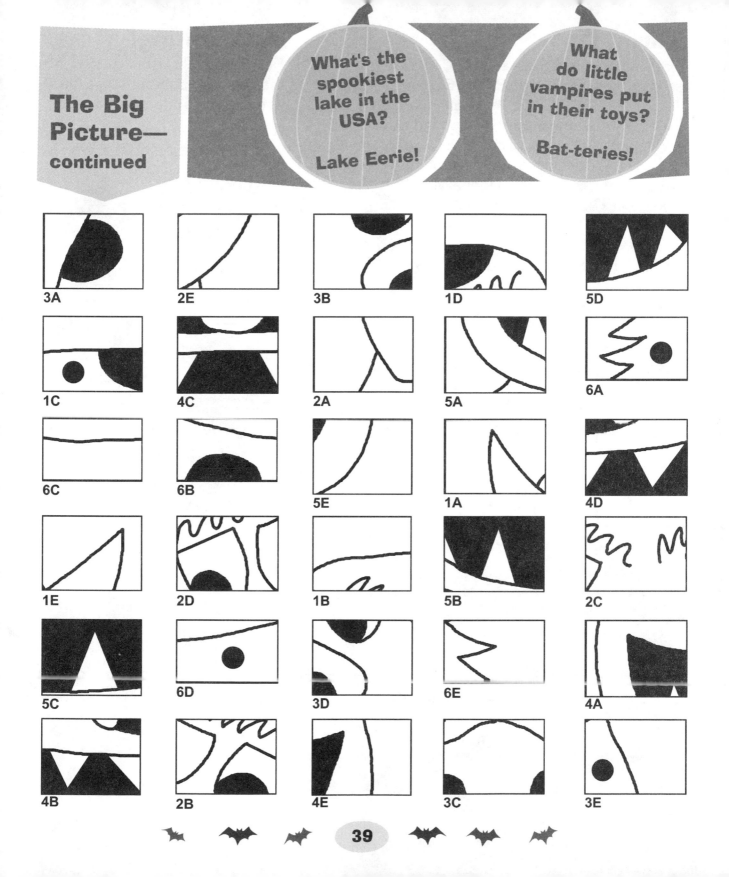

3A

2E

3B

1D

5D

1C

4C

2A

5A

6A

6C

6B

5E

1A

4D

1E

2D

1B

5B

2C

5C

6D

3D

6E

4A

4B

2B

4E

3C

3E

Movin' On

This zombie wants to leave town. Can you lead him from his **GRAVESTONE** to the **RAILROAD**? Travel one space at a time making compound words as you go. You can move up and down and side to side—but *not* diagonally!

GRAVE	YARD	WORK	HORSE
STONE	STICK	HAND	BALL
WALL	PAPER	BACK	YARD
BACK	CLIP	HAND	RAIL
BONE	WHITE	BACK	ROAD

Why is a cemetery the best place to write a novel?

Because there are a lot of plots there!

Just Joking!

Fill in the blanks with the answers to the following questions. Use the letters at the bottom of the page.

What would you name a monster with no arms and no legs who is . . .

...FLOATING IN A POOL?

_ _ _

...HANGING ON A WALL?

_ _ _

...LYING BY A DOOR?

_ _ _ _

M a t B r
t A o t b

40

Fright Night

Fill in the triangles on the screen to see what scary movie these kids are watching.

Grandmonster

This monster is having a birthday. How old is he going to be? Find all the numbers hidden in the following sentences. Then add them up and you'll know how old he is.

1) How often do neat women clean?

2) It won't snow into next week.

3) The freight train won't enter the station until six o'clock.

4) Pat won three gymnastic medals even after falling down.

5) Seth reeked after camping for two weeks.

6) I'm sorry if I've gone away for too long.

7) Kate needs to lose weight.

8) If our cat won't be careful, he will lose one of his nine lives.

TOTAL:

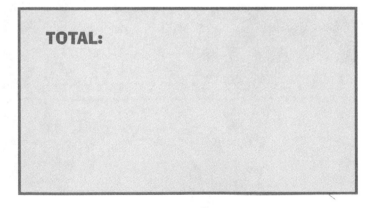

Monster Mama

Little monsters may look similar to us, but each monster mamma knows her own special baby! Can you pick out and circle the one baby that belongs to each mama?

Extra, Extra

Answer as many clues as you can and fill the letters into the grid. Work back and forth between the box and the clues. When you are finished, you will know the answer to the riddle.

Where does a lady monster keep her spare parts?

1F	2F	3B		4A K	5C	6F	7A P	8F		
9E	10B	11A E	12D		13E	14B		15E	16A E	17C
18D	19C	20E	21F	22C	23D	24C				

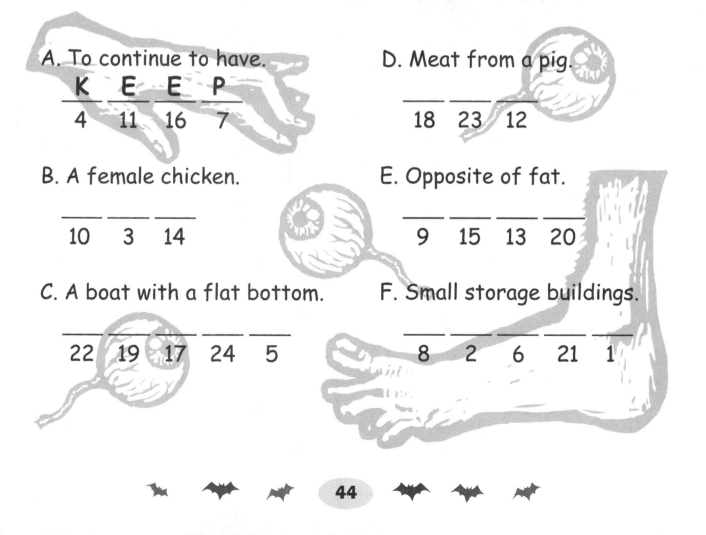

A. To continue to have.

K E E P
4 11 16 7

B. A female chicken.

___ ___ ___
10 3 14

C. A boat with a flat bottom.

___ ___ ___ ___ ___
22 19 17 24 5

D. Meat from a pig.

___ ___ ___
18 23 12

E. Opposite of fat.

___ ___ ___ ___
9 15 13 20

F. Small storage buildings.

___ ___ ___ ___ ___
8 2 6 21 1

44

Mixed-Up Monsters

Here's a great game that you can play with one or two friends. Three players works best.

You will need: **white drawing paper, scissors, and pencils.**

1.

Cut the paper in half the long way.

Each player gets one strip of paper. Fold the paper strip in thirds.

2.

Each player draws a head. Don't let anyone see your drawing!

Make pencil marks in the next box to show where the neck goes.

3.

Fold head under. Switch papers. Each player draws a body. Remember, don't let anyone see your drawing!

Make marks in the last box to show where the legs go.

4.

Fold body under. Switch papers. Each player draws legs and feet.

5.

When everyone is finished, unfold the papers to see your mixed-up monsters! Can you come up with funny names for them?

The Big-Eyed Chickosquid

Double Up

This two-headed monster wants to see if you can fill all the double-letter words into the crossword grid on the next page. Award yourself a good **H-O-W-L** if you get the word that has three pairs of double letters!

ACROSS

1. Sweaty season
3. Greedy
6. Sorry!
7. To wed
9. Hang loosely
11. Sodas do it
13. Not the same
14. Bright with light
17. Also
18. Nail hitter
19. Keep balls in the air
20. Kind of movie
21. Spicy spice
23. Accountant
27. Kanga's baby
28. Person in charge
29. Not warm
32. Ghost costume
33. You knock on it
34. Say yes
35. Not neat
37. Ice cream server
39. Blow a horn
40. Use someone else's
41. Curly haired dog
42. Tasty
44. Caterpillar's home
45. Small fish

DOWN

2. Thief
4. Little laugh
5. Dog noise
8. Tricky joke
9. Not the top
10. Anteater
12. Not outside
15. Sliced milk
16. Less shallow
20. Boy wizard
22. Written messages
23. Soapy sphere
24. X
25. Lovely looking
26. Masked mammal
30. Climber's helper
31. Teacher's place
35. Wrapped monster
36. Go after
38. Weird
39. Stomach
43. Cow noise

What kind of noise does a ghost owl make?

Boo hoot, Boo hoot!

They can't do it!

Sure they can!

Monster Merge

Choose pairs of words from the word list. Merge them together to create strange, new words that answer the question:

What do you get when you cross . . .

STEINWAY

WIZARD

MOO

COLA

ZILLION

FRANKENSTEIN

DRACULA

AARDVARK

GODZILLA

MONSTER

SNACK

... a monster and a cow?

A " M O O S T E R "

... a mad scientist and a famous piano?

A " _ R _ N _ E _ S _ E _ N _ _ _ "

... a monster and a lot of money?

A " _ O _ _ _ _ _ _ O N "

... junk food and a vampire?

" S N _ _ _ _ _ _ "

... a vampire and a soda?

" _ R _ _ O _ _ "

... a male witch and an anteater?

A " _ _ _ _ _ R _ _ _ R _ "

HINT: The first one is done, and we've left some M-O-N-S-T-E-R-S to help you out! Words from the list may be used more than once.

48

Chapter 5

All Dressed Up

Bits and Pieces

Here are close-up drawings of nine different Halloween costumes. Can you tell what each one is? Write the answers below.

1. _____
2. _____
3. _____
4. _____
5. _____
6. _____
7. _____
8. _____
9. _____

Family Fun

Each member of the Murphy family has a different costume, but they are all using the same theme. Unscramble each costume name and write it in the grid. Then read the shaded blocks to discover the Murphy family theme!

1. IORBN _____
2. ONILFAMG _____
3. KOSTR _____
4. CUDK _____
5. AWSN _____

What's That You Say?

What kind of character might say the following phrases? Figure each one out and you'll be able to fill in the criss-cross. We left you some **C-O-S-T-U-M-E-S** to help you out.

"Ahoy, Matey"

"I hate kissing frogs!"

"Giddy-up!"

"If I only had a brain!"

"I vant to drink your blood!"

"Please don't pick me!"

"Boo!"

"Take me to your leader."

"It's chilly with no skin on."

"Blast off!"

"I'm all wrapped up!"

"I'll turn you into a toad!"

"Strike!"

"I smell smoke!"

"I love the full moon!"

"Let me tell your fortune."

"Where's my magic lamp?"

"I dance on my toes!"

"I'm soooo funny!"

"Woof!"

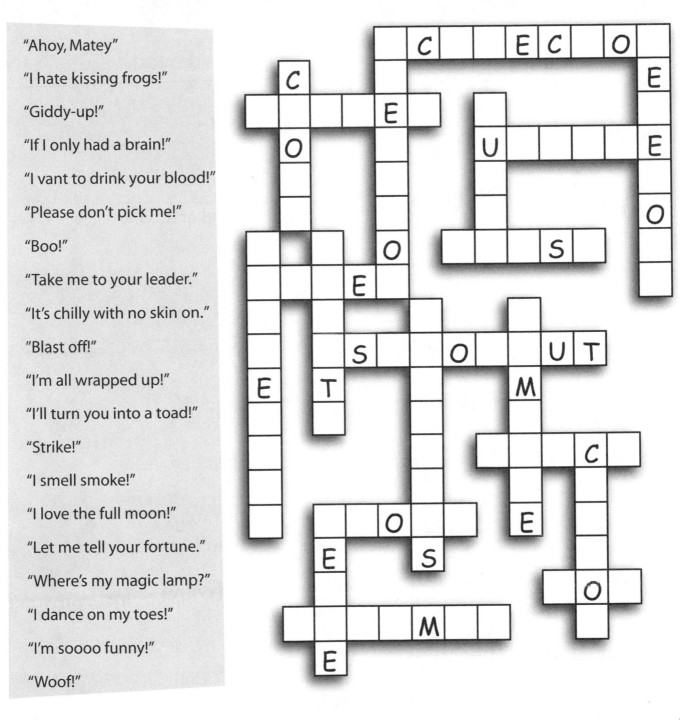

Dress Him Up

Fill in each blank using the clues. Then, read the description of each item and draw it onto the boy. When you're finished, what is his costume?

1. A _____ around his head.
   large, square scarf that's often red

2. A _____ on one shoulder.
   large, green bird that can talk

3. Instead of one hand, he has a _____.
   it's on the end of a fishing line

4. A big hoop _____ in one ear.
   jewelry for the ear

5. A black _____ over one eye.
   it covers a hole in your jeans

6. A big, black _____.
   hair that grows under a man's nose

7. Pair of tall, black _____.
   rubber foot covers you wear in the rain

8. A long, thin _____ on his face.
   mark on the skin after a cut

9. A long _____ hangs from his belt.
   weapon with a flat, metal blade

10. Long, black, stringy _____.
    it grows on top of your head

Quick Change

At the last minute, Olivia was invited to a costume party. Start with the word **SHEET**, and change one letter on each of the lines so that you end up with the word **GHOST**. Now Olivia will have something to wear to the party!

HINT: The words you make will not be real words!

SHEET

_____

_____

_____

GHOST

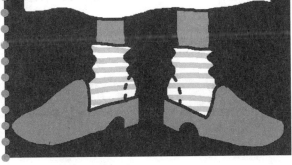

Mirror, Mirror

Christa wonders if the other kids at the Halloween party will like her costume. To find out, start at the letter S marked with a dot. Move in a clockwise direction and collect every other letter until you come back to where you started. Write those letters into the answer blanks. Then, go around the frame again and collect all the letters you missed the first time.

HINT: Cross the letters out as you go around the frame!

Frame letters (top): ˙S S O C M O E S K T I U

Frame letters (right, top to bottom): D M S E W A I N L D L

Frame letters (bottom, left to right): I C W E E K M I O L S

Frame letters (left, top to bottom): A T T O S N I L R L H

__ __ __ __   __ __ __ __

__ __ __ __   __ __ __ __

__ __ __ __ __ __ '

__ __ __ __ __ __ ,

__ __ __ __ __ __

__ __ __ __ __ __ !

What to Wear?

There are so many choices when it comes to dressing up on Halloween. You could pick any number of the following items to help create a fabulous costume. But can you find them all in this word search? Remember, they can run up or down, backward or forward—even diagonally! **Bonus:** when you're done, read the unused letters to discover how much money is spent every year on Halloween costumes.

ANTENNA
BADGE
BANDANA
BEARD
BIG FEET

BOA
BOOTS
BOWTIE
BROOM
CAPE

CAULDRON
CROWN

EARRINGS
EARS
EYEPATCH
FANGS
FINGERNAILS

FLOWER
GLASSES
GOWN
HAT
HELMET

HOLSTER
HORNS
MAKEUP
MASK
MUSTACHE
NOSE
PINWHEEL
SCAR
SHEET
SLIPPERS
SWORD
TAIL
TUTU
WAND
WART
WHISKERS
WIG
WINGS

```
E E O T M E N E A E S O N S R A
G H A N E O A W A N D D T E N P
S L C R S E O R A H A O W A U L
L S A A R L F R S F O O D E N E
I B G S T I I G B B L N K O P N
P A T N S S N A I F A A R A W I
P O A H I E U G N B M D C O L L
E B I A I W S M S R L F G O G U
R K L T N D R L E U E B A O I T
S S L L N E E Y A A B G E N W U
A A R W T E E C H H N O N A G T
S M O S H P E O S T E N W I R S
I R L W A G R W S S E L E T F D
C O N T D N O W A R T E M T I P
H I C A S R S C A R E N H E N E
P H B T D W H I S K E R S S T A
```

HINT: Cross each word off the list after you have found it.

Costly Costumes

Annie has $15 to spend on her Halloween costume. Browse through the shelves of the store on the next page and see if you can find *everything* for each of her costume choices. When you've found it all, add up each column and see what Annie will be for Halloween!

HINT: Some items can be used more than once.

WITCH	Clown	Ballerina	Cowgirl
_____	_____	_____	_____
_____	_____	_____	_____
_____	_____	_____	_____
_____	_____	_____	_____
_____	_____	_____	_____
_____	_____	_____	_____
_____	_____	_____	_____
_____	_____	_____	_____
_____	_____	_____	_____
_____	_____	_____	_____
_____	_____	_____	_____

Many Masks

The masks on this wall look very similar, but the one that Brian wants is unique. Can you find it?

Brian's mask has *all* of the following features:

one eye open, one closed   5 feathers   big nose

frowning mouth   pattern that looks like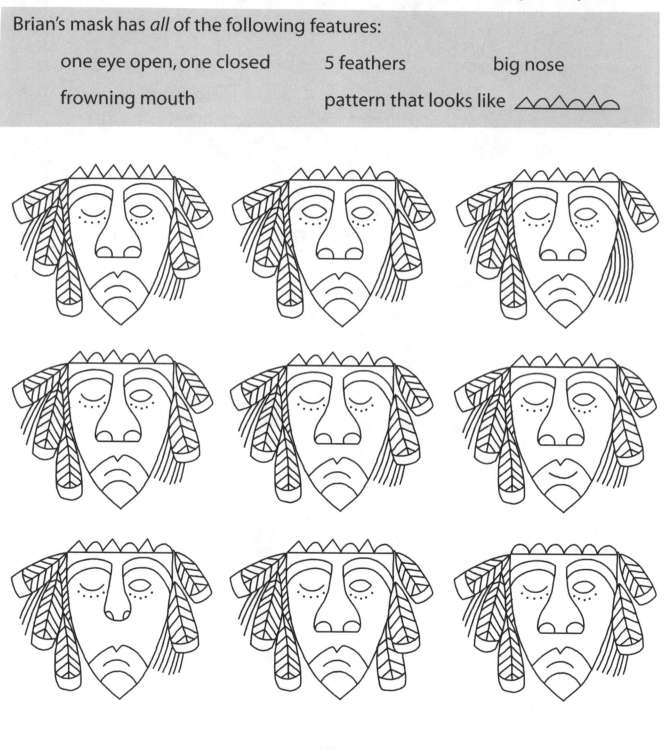

All Wrapped Up!

Tommy was dying to be a mummy for Halloween. His Dad helped out by wrapping him from head to toe in toilet paper. Can you find your way from **START** to **END**?

START

Mumbling Mummy

Fill in the missing letters for all these words that rhyme with MUMMY.

Sticky and chewy.
__UMMY

Another word for stomach.
__UMMY

Not very good.
__ __UMMY

Delicious!
__UMMY

END

What's Dot?

Start at number 1 and connect the dots to see what Dorothy will be for Halloween.

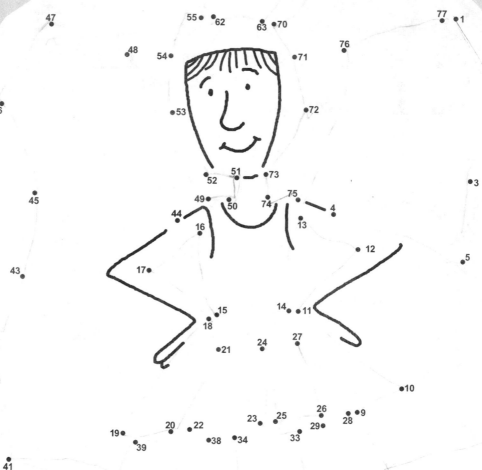

What is evil on the inside, and orange on the outside?

A witch dressed as a pumpkin!

Perfect Timing

Halloween would be a perfect time for a real alien to sneak onto Earth—who would notice? See if you can figure out who (or what) the real alien is in this group of trick-or-treaters.

a. Kelly does not have three antennae.

b. Both Ethan and Olivia both have scales.

c. Peter is standing next to the alien with webbed feet.

d. Olivia does not have two heads.

Taking Treats

The same five "aliens" from the puzzle above were the last trick-or-treaters at the Hudson house. There were 15 treats when they got there, and no treats after they left. How many treats did each alien take? Use the clues to figure it out.

Each trick-or-treater took at least one treat.

Kelly took two treats less than Olivia.

Ethan took four treats.

Peter and Olivia took the same number of treats.

The real alien took one treat more than Peter.

Olivia took one treat less than Ethan.

Looking for Letters

Follow the letters to spell out what trick-or-treaters might chant as they go door to door on Halloween.

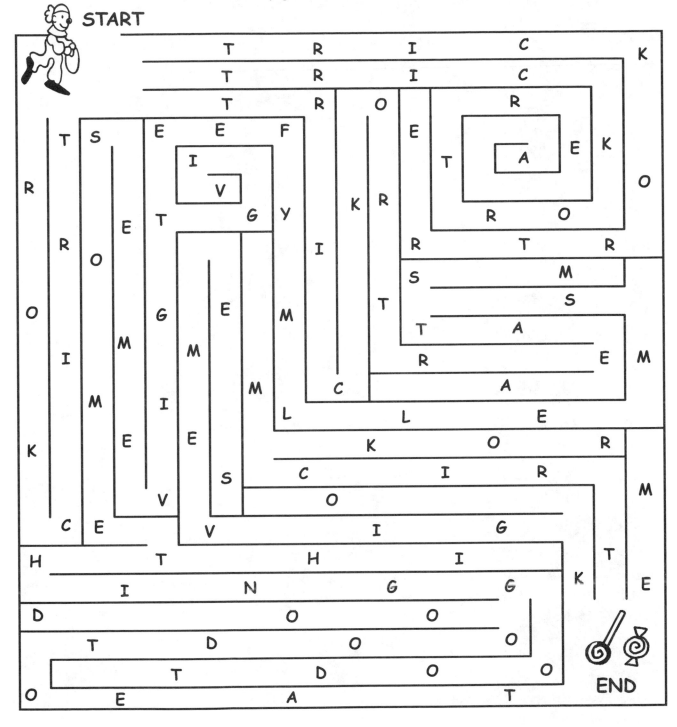

START

END

Short Cut

Are you sure this is the right way home? See if you can find the path.

House to House

Can you get from house to house in this puzzle? You must travel one space at a time, making compound words as you go. You can move up and down, and side to side—but not diagonally!

HOUSE	WORK	PLACE	MAT	OPEN
BOAT	HOUSE	FLY	AWAY	SKY
BACK	HOLD	PAPER	WEIGHT	LESS
ACHE	UP	BACK	YARD	STICK
COOL	WIND	FIRE	WOOD	STOVE
DOWN	FALL	SIDE	WIND	FALL
POUR	SLOW	PITCH	BLACK	OUT
HAND	BOOK	CASE	LOAD	HOUSE

Under Wraps

An important reminder about candy that you get when trick-or-treating is hidden in this mint. To read it, start at the arrow and spiral into the middle using every other letter. When you hit the center, spiral back out, using all the letters that you missed.

Trick or Treat?

In the list below are both tricks and treats—in which grid will you find these words? Tricks are hiding in the grid on the **left**, and treats are on the **right**. Words can run forward, backward, up, down, or diagonally. Why not use two different color markers to highlight each word as you find it?

CANDY APPLE
CANDY CORN
CHOCOLATE
BAR
CIDER
CUPCAKE
DONUT
FAKE SPIDER
GUM
HIDING

JOKE
KNOCKING
LICORICE
LOLLIPOP

MAGIC TRICK
MONEY
PENCIL
PEPPERMINT
POPCORN BALL
PRANK
RIDDLE

RING DOORBELL
ROTTEN EGG
SCARY NOISE
SCREAM

SHAVING CREAM
SILLY STRING
SOAP
STICKER
TAFFY
TIP GARBAGE
CAN
TOILET PAPER
TOY
UGLY FACE

T	O	I	L	E	T	P	A	P	E	R
W	P	N	J	O	K	E	U	R	X	I
N	X	S	I	N	N	I	G	A	Q	N
K	O	H	P	A	O	S	L	N	P	G
C	N	A	R	C	C	C	Y	K	S	D
I	F	V	J	E	K	R	F	S	I	O
R	A	I	O	G	I	E	A	I	L	O
T	K	N	K	A	N	A	C	L	L	R
C	E	G	L	B	G	M	E	L	Y	B
I	S	C	A	R	Y	N	O	I	S	E
G	P	R	P	A	P	P	L	O	T	L
A	I	E	O	G	T	R	I	C	R	L
M	D	A	V	P	G	N	I	D	I	H
T	E	M	R	I	D	D	L	E	N	X
X	R	O	T	T	E	N	E	G	G	L

Y	W	X	L	I	C	O	R	I	C	E
M	O	N	E	Y	P	E	P	P	P	X
Q	M	T	U	N	O	D	S	O	E	W
R	X	T	S	Y	P	O	X	P	P	Q
A	I	M	F	S	C	Q	T	I	P	O
B	C	F	C	L	O	G	U	L	E	S
E	A	O	N	M	R	X	O	L	R	T
T	N	K	R	O	N	R	P	O	M	I
A	X	Q	O	N	B	P	C	L	I	C
L	O	E	C	W	A	E	N	W	N	K
O	R	X	Y	Y	L	N	X	I	T	E
C	A	N	D	L	L	C	I	D	E	R
O	C	N	N	O	R	I	X	G	U	W
H	A	O	A	L	O	L	L	U	I	Q
C	U	P	C	A	K	E	O	M	C	X

Coin-Incidentally

In many parts of our country, children trick-or-treat for money to give to needy children rather than for candy for themselves. By using the coin code below, figure out the name of the organization that sponsors this tradition. **HINT:** The answer is an "acronym," which is a word formed from the first letters of other words.

Code: A=1 cent, B=2 cents, C=3 cents, etc.

Can I collect coins for this organization, too?

Sure! Have a parent call 1-800-252-KIDS to find out how to get your own coin box!

Lights Out!

What time is trick-or-treating over in this neighborhood? To find out, solve the equations below and cross out the luminaries containing the answers. Add the numbers in the remaining luminaries and you will know what time everybody heads home.

Witch Walk

Follow the directions below to see which words on the walkway you should cross out. Read the remaining words from top to bottom to find the answer to this riddle:

What did the little witch hope to get when she went trick-or-treating?

$6 + 4 =$ ___

$8 - 3 =$ ___

$2 + 5 =$ ___

$7 + 2 =$ ___

$4 + 4 =$ ___

$5 - 4 =$ ___

$3 + 3 =$ ___

$6 - 2 =$ ___

$2 + 2 =$ ___

$4 - 1 =$ ___

Cross out all the words that start **or** end with D **or** Y.

Cross out all the words that have the letter U.

Luminaries: 1, 3, 4, 2, 2, 3, 5, 9, 1, 7, 6, 4, 8, 10

Walkway words: SHE DID HAD YOU WAS UP HOPING FOR FOOD WANTED GLAD WISHED A DOLLAR DO GOOD CHARM AND MANY FUN BRACELET CANDY

Safety Matters

There are some common sense rules you should follow when you are out trick-or-treating. Unscramble the letters of the mystery words and match them to the correct sentence. They will remind you how to stay safe while you are having fun!

TULDA = _____

THIGLS = _____

LAWK = _____

OYU ANKTH = _____

GINTEA = _____

THIGSHLAFL = _____

FLEMA = _____

GRNATSRES = _____

REVEN = _____

BROODHOGONEI = _____

1. Young children should always trick-or-treat

   with an _____.

2. _____ trick-or-treat by yourself!

3. Wear a _____ - retardant costume.

4. Check candy before _____ it.

5. Only visit houses with the _____ on.

6. Always carry a _____ at night.

7. Don't forget to say "_____ _____".

Scared Skeleton

To find out the solution to the question below, answer as many clues as you can. Put the letters into the grid. Work back and forth between the box and the clues until you have the answer to this riddle.

Why didn't the little skeleton cross the road to trick-or-treat?

A. Nickname for Theodore

$\dfrac{T}{8}$ $\dfrac{E}{15}$ $\dfrac{D}{3}$

B. Home for a bee

$\overline{}_{1}$ $\overline{}_{4}$ $\overline{}_{11}$ $\overline{}_{2}$

C. A large mound of sand

$\overline{}_{5}$ $\overline{}_{17}$ $\overline{}_{6}$ $\overline{}_{12}$

D. Item worn on the head

$\overline{}_{9}$ $\overline{}_{10}$ $\overline{}_{18}$

E. Spirit of a dead person

$\overline{}_{16}$ $\overline{}_{14}$ $\overline{}_{7}$ $\overline{}_{19}$ $\overline{}_{13}$

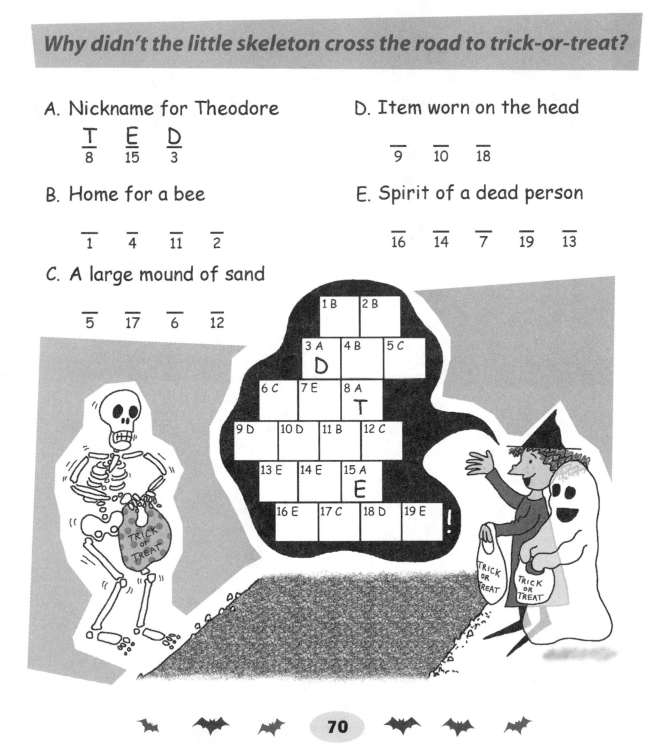

1 B	2 B

3 A	4 B	5 C
D		

6 C	7 E	8 A
		T

9 D	10 D	11 B	12 C

13 E	14 E	15 A
		E

16 E	17 C	18 D	19 E

Sorting the Loot

You've dumped out your trick-or-treat bag. Now see if you can answer the following questions:

- How many different kinds of treats are there?
- Which treat was given the most?
- Which is your favorite treat?
- Of which treat is there only one?
- How much do the coins add up to?
- Are there more spider rings or swirly mints?

Windy Night

Can you find the following 14 costume pieces scattered in this garden? COWBOY HAT, FAIRY WAND, BROOM, WITCH HAT, GHOST, ANGEL'S HALO, CLOWN MASK, DARK GLASSES, BUTTERFLY WINGS, CLOWN SHOE, CAT EARS, WITCH NOSE, MAGICIAN'S CLOAK, STOCKING CAP.

Chapter 7

You're Invited

Where's the Party?

You just received a strange invitation in the mail. Can you figure out what it says—and who sent it to you?

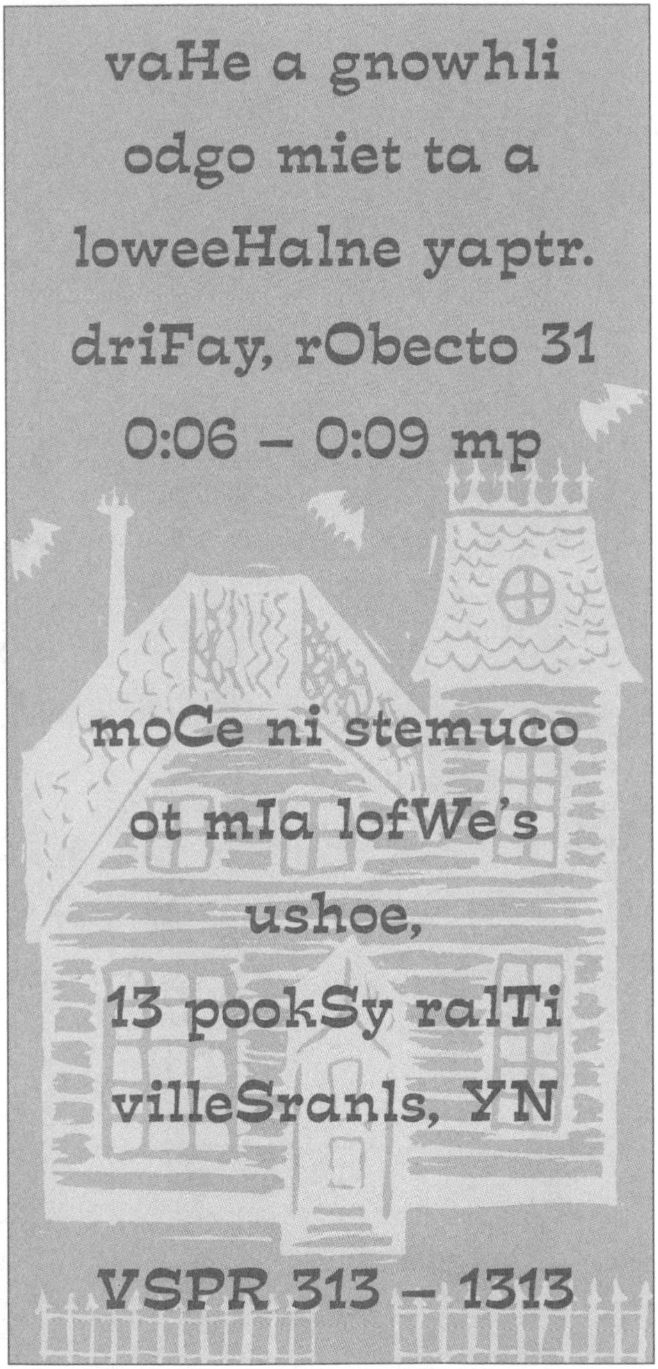

vaHe a gnowhli
odgo miet ta a
loweeHalne yaptr.
driFay, rObecto 31
0:06 – 0:09 mp
moCe ni stemuco
ot mIa lofWe's
ushoe,
13 pookSy ralTi
villeSranls, YN
VSPR 313 – 1313

The back of the invitation has directions to the house. Use the decoder to figure out exactly where the party is!

A B C D E
F G H I J
K L M N O
P Q R S T
U V W X Y

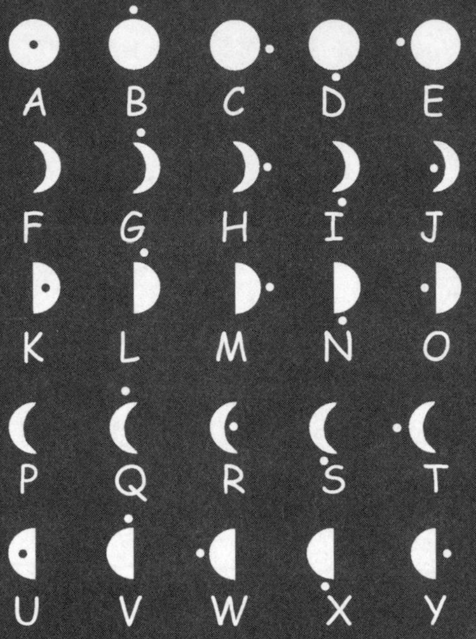

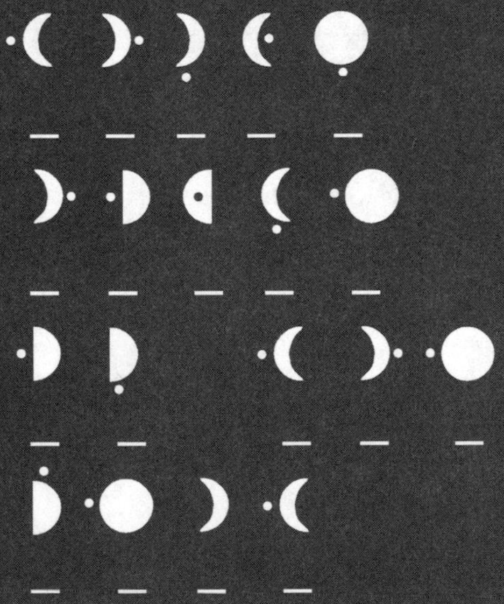

Donut on a String

The letters inside these donuts can read forward or backward. Unfortunately, someone has taken a bite out of each donut and a letter is missing! See if you can figure out the different types.

Bobbing for Apples

Take the letters in each apple and write them in the missing spaces of each word to create words that fit each clue. Use each apple only once. You will end up with six words that all start with **B-O-B**.

BO _ _ IN .... a spool for winding thread

BO _ _ AT .... a small wildcat

BO _ _ LED .... a long sled for racing

BO _ _ HITE .... a bird that makes a sound like its name

BO _ _ IE .... a nickname for a girl named Roberta

Perfect Plans

Ryan had all the plans for his Halloween party in a notebook. Unfortunately, his little sister ripped out the pages! Help Ryan get organized by writing the proper page number on each page.

c

ri

o

pk

Ask mom and Dad if party is O.K.!!!
Choose day.
Make guest list.

Send Invitations
What costume?
Plan food and games

op

pp

Find stuff for costume
Make food
Carve Pumpkins

e

Put on Costume
Put snacks on table
Greet Guests

ll

Hang balloons
Set table
Set up games

a

Buy (make?) Decorations
Pick pumpkins
Go to market

or

c

u

Oh, no! Ryan's little sister has been at it again! Now she's removed half the letters from his shopping list. Fix the list by using letters scattered on this page.

p_p_r_ups   st__ng

a__les   d_n_ts

_ider   na__ins

_a__oons   p__c__n

Ooey Gooey

Have you ever played this popular Halloween game? Everyone covers their eyes while a "mad scientist" passes around bowls containing the "body parts" he will use to make his next monster. **Gross! What is that stuff?** Unscramble the words in the ingredients list. See which monster part each is a good substitute for. Write each ingredient in the spaces provided. Don't forget to wash your hands when you're done!

EYEBALLS = peeled _ _ _ _ _ _ _

NOSE = piece of _ _ _ _ _ _ _

TEETH = _ _ _ _ _ _ _ _ _ _

HAIR = fresh _ _ _ _ _ _ _

BRAIN = cooked _ _ _ _ _ _ _ _ _ _ _

BONES = broken _ _ _ _ _ _ _ _ _

FINGERNAILS = _ _ _ _ _ _ _ _ _ _

FINGER = old, limp _ _ _ _ _ _ _

GUTS = cooked, oiled _ _ _ _ _ _ _ _ _ _ _

HEART = peeled _ _ _ _ _ _ _

CSABRNHE

IETASPGHT

SUOPSRT

TRRCAO

SLSTNUHEL

OAMTOT

DOHTOG

EPRGAS

OYACNDRCN

WEFUCALILOR

Name the Game

Nine little ghosts are out in the yard playing a party game. Follow the directions to fill in the squares and find out what game they are playing.

1
2
3
4
5
6
7
8
9

1. Fill in all the blocks on the left side of all the ghosts.

2. Fill in all the blocks across the top of ghosts 1, 2, 3, 5, 6, 7, and 9.

3. Fill in all the blocks across the bottom for ghosts 1, 2, 3, 5, and 9.

4. Fill in all the blocks on the right side for ghosts 2, 3, 4, 7, and 8.

5. Fill in just the center block for ghosts 1, 4, 5, and 7.

6. Fill in all the blocks across the middle row of ghost 6.

7. Fill in the fourth block from the top in the right hand column of ghost 9.

Halloween Hangman

TO PLAY: You need two people, paper, and a pencil.

Player 1 draws the gallows. Then he or she thinks up a secret word, and puts the correct number of spaces under the gallows. **Player 1** is allowed to give hints about the secret word, like, "It's a costume," or, "It's a spooky sound."

Player 2 guesses one letter at a time. If the letter *is* in the secret word, **Player 1** writes it in the proper space. If the letter *is not* in the word, **Player 1** writes the used letter above the gallows, and draws a head on the hangman.

Player 2 continues to guess letters, one at a time. Each time a correct letter is guessed, it gets added in its proper space to spell out the secret word. Each time a wrong letter is guessed, a new body part is added to the hangman. Body parts include: head, body, arms, legs, eyes, nose, and a frown.

TO WIN: If **Player 2** guesses the secret word before the hangman is completely drawn, he or she wins. If all the body parts are drawn on the hangman before **Player 2** has guessed the secret word, **Player 1** wins. At any time, **Player 2** can try to guess the whole word, but automatically loses the game if the guess is wrong.

FOR YOUNGER PLAYERS: Adding hands, feet, ears, hair, and even fingers and toes to the hangman gives younger players many more chances to guess letters!

Oops! Player 2 in this game did not guess the word "spooky" before the hangman was completely drawn. **Player 1** wins.

GALLOWS

F L R
M T A

S _ _ O O _

Try playing this game using only spooky Halloween words. Here's a list to choose from:

GHOST	BLACK CAT
CEMETERY	GRAVESTONE
BROOMSTICK	VAMPIRE
CAULDRON	CREEPY
MONSTER	SKELETON
WARLOCK	ZOMBIE

Solitaire Hangman

Above each word grid is a Halloween theme. Use one letter from each column to spell a word that goes with the theme. Each time you can't spell a word and have to start again in the first column, add another part to the hangman. One word has been done for you.

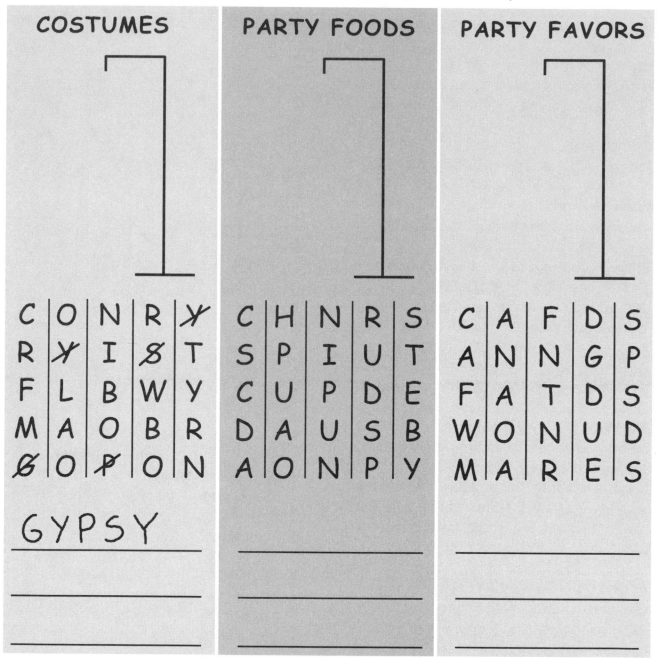

COSTUMES

C	O	N	R	~~Y~~
R	~~Y~~	I	~~S~~	T
F	L	B	W	Y
M	A	O	B	R
~~G~~	O	~~P~~	O	N

GYPSY

PARTY FOODS

C	H	N	R	S
S	P	I	U	T
C	U	P	D	E
D	A	U	S	B
A	O	N	P	Y

PARTY FAVORS

C	A	F	D	S
A	N	N	G	P
F	A	T	D	S
W	O	N	U	D
M	A	R	E	S

In each grid, there are three or four possible answers to the question.
Can you get more than one answer before the hangman's time is up?

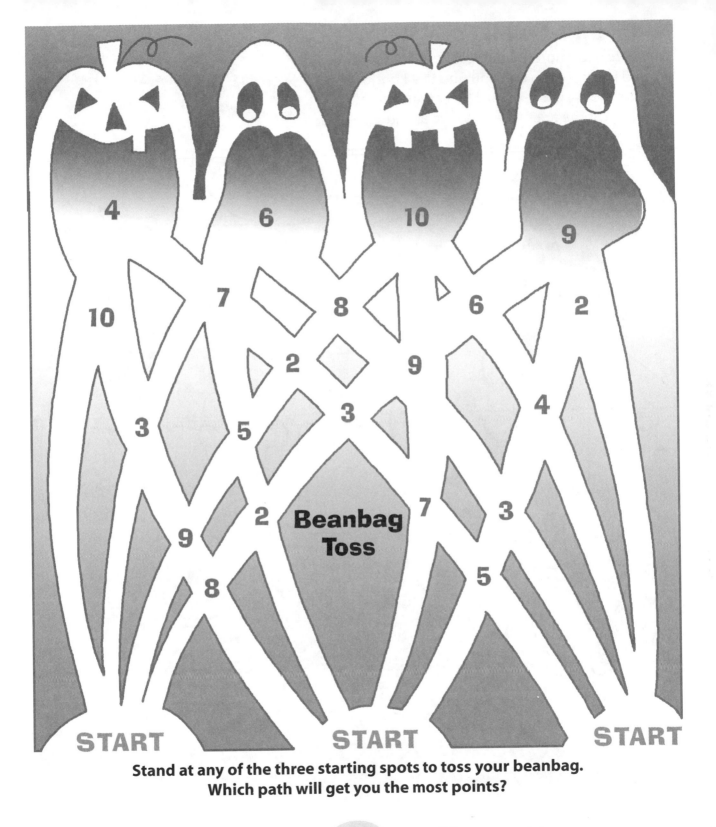

Stand at any of the three starting spots to toss your beanbag.
Which path will get you the most points?

Hide and Seek

There are a lot more than apples bobbing around in this party. Can you find the 12 ghosts who are hiding in the room? Be careful—they are tricky. Some are tiny, and some are huge!

What kind of ghosts cheer at football games?

School spirits!

Ghost Bowling

Which of these kids at the party scored the highest? Add only the points on the ghost pins that were knocked over.

EXTRA: If each kid gets another turn and knocks over two more pins, what's the *most* each player can score?

Debbie

Josh

Maxine

Face Painting

It's always fun to put on colorful makeup when getting dressed for a Halloween party! To complete this costume, you will need colored pencils or crayons. Using the correct color, shade in the numbered boxes that are listed for each row (remember, rows go across). Be sure to fill in each box carefully from left to right. **SPECIAL DIRECTIONS:** If there is a set of numbers with a dash between them (for example 5-16), that means you must shade in box 5, box 16, *and* all the numbers in between!

▶ Color all numbered boxes from LEFT to RIGHT across the grid.

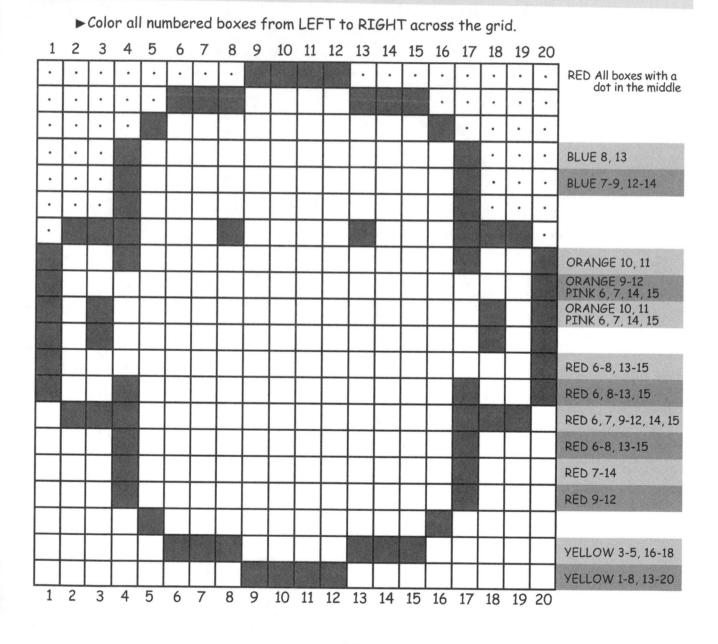

RED All boxes with a dot in the middle

BLUE 8, 13

BLUE 7-9, 12-14

ORANGE 10, 11

ORANGE 9-12
PINK 6, 7, 14, 15

ORANGE 10, 11
PINK 6, 7, 14, 15

RED 6-8, 13-15

RED 6, 8-13, 15

RED 6, 7, 9-12, 14, 15

RED 6-8, 13-15

RED 7-14

RED 9-12

YELLOW 3-5, 16-18

YELLOW 1-8, 13-20

Where in the World?

Everyone knows that chocolate comes from the local supermarket—or does it? Answer as many clues below as you can, and fill the letters you have into the grid. Work back and forth between the grid and clues until you discover where your favorite treat really comes from! **HINT:** One word has been done for you.

1 Q	2 I	3 Q	4 O	5 L	6 O	7 G	8 N	9 C		10 M	11 L	12 I	13 G	14 F	
15 L	16 C	17 B	18 R		19 J	20 K	21 G	22 K	23 M		24 Q	25 R	26 O	27 P	28 N
	29 D	30 D	31 H	32 H		33 N	34 F	35 M		36 E	37 K	38 B	39 O	40 C	
41 A O	42 N		43 H	44 J	45 B	46 E	47 E		48 I	49 G	50 A E	51 C	52 M		
53 N	54 H		55 K	56 F	57 F		58 A T	59 E	60 A O	61 M	62 E	63 B	64 D	65 E	
66 A R	67 J	68 C	69 P	70 B	71 B	72 A S		73 F	74 J		75 G	76 H	77 M		
78 D	79 I	80 A R	81 E	82 L											

A. A male chicken.

$\underline{R}$ $\underline{O}$ $\underline{O}$ $\underline{S}$ $\underline{T}$ $\underline{E}$ $\underline{R}$
66   60   41   72   58   50   80

B. Silky caterpillar case.

$\underline{}$ $\underline{}$ $\underline{}$ $\underline{}$ $\underline{}$ $\underline{}$
63   70   45   38   17   71

C. Color of grass.

$\underline{}$ $\underline{}$ $\underline{}$ $\underline{}$ $\underline{}$
68   16   51   9   40

D. To melt.

$\underline{}$ $\underline{}$ $\underline{}$ $\underline{}$
29   30   64   78

E. A large ape.

$\underline{}$ $\underline{}$ $\underline{}$ $\underline{}$ $\underline{}$ $\underline{}$ $\underline{}$
36   47   59   62   65   81   46

F. Land on the edge of the ocean.

$\underline{}$ $\underline{}$ $\underline{}$ $\underline{}$ $\underline{}$
14   56   73   34   57

G. Copy lines through a thin piece of paper.

$\underline{}$ $\underline{}$ $\underline{}$ $\underline{}$ $\underline{}$
75   49   7   21   13

H. Repeat words over and over.

$\underline{}$ $\underline{}$ $\underline{}$ $\underline{}$ $\underline{}$
43   76   31   54   32

I. Insect that looks like a butterfly.

$\underline{}$ $\underline{}$ $\underline{}$ $\underline{}$
12   79   48   2

J. Front of the head.

$\underline{}$ $\underline{}$ $\underline{}$ $\underline{}$
74   44   19   67

K. Plant part that grows underground.

$$\overline{37} \ \overline{22} \ \overline{20} \ \overline{55}$$

L. What you eat.

$$\overline{15} \ \overline{11} \ \overline{5} \ \overline{82}$$

M. To get away.

$$\overline{35} \ \overline{52} \ \overline{10} \ \overline{23} \ \overline{61} \ \overline{77}$$

N. A dirty spot on clothing.

$$\overline{28} \ \overline{8} \ \overline{33} \ \overline{53} \ \overline{42}$$

O. Sharp, curved nail on an animal.

$$\overline{4} \ \overline{6} \ \overline{26} \ \overline{39}$$

P. Opposite of out.

$$\overline{69} \ \overline{27}$$

Q. What's left when you eat fresh corn.

$$\overline{1} \ \overline{3} \ \overline{24}$$

R. Opposite of you.

$$\overline{18} \ \overline{25}$$

Wherever it comes from, it's YUM!

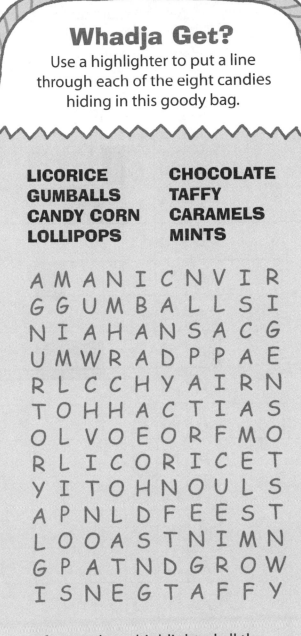

Whadja Get?

Use a highlighter to put a line through each of the eight candies hiding in this goody bag.

LICORICE **CHOCOLATE**
GUMBALLS **TAFFY**
CANDY CORN **CARAMELS**
LOLLIPOPS **MINTS**

```
A M A N I C N V I R
G G U M B A L L S I
N I A H A N S A C G
U M W R A D P P A E
R L C C H Y A I R N
T O H H A C T I A S
O L V O E O R F M O
R L I C O R I C E T
Y I T O H N O U L S
A P N L D F E E S T
L O O A S T N I M N
G P A T N D G R O W
I S N E G T A F F Y
```

After you have highlighted all the candy, read the leftover letters from left to right and top to bottom. You will find an absolutely amazing fact!

Dandy Candy

All the words in this puzzle contain the letters **A-N-D**.
Figure out each new word from the clues provided.

D	A	N	D	Y

	A	N	D		

China's black and white bear.

	A	N	D				

Good-looking man.

			A	N	D	

Ask for forcefully.

	A	N	D			

Like a beach or desert.

		A	N	D		

The son of your son.

	A	N	D		

Walk with no place to go.

	A	N	D		

By chance or accident.

	A	N	D			

Human-looking robot.

		A	N	D	

Land surrounded by water.

	A	N	D			

Person who destroys propety.

	A	N	D				

Cloth used to cover a wound.

	A	N	D			

One who rents apartments.

	A	N	D			

Meat between sliced bread.

C	A	N	D	Y

Favorite Flavor

Do you know what kind of candy is America's favorite? If you fill in all the **Y-U-Ms**, it will become very clear.

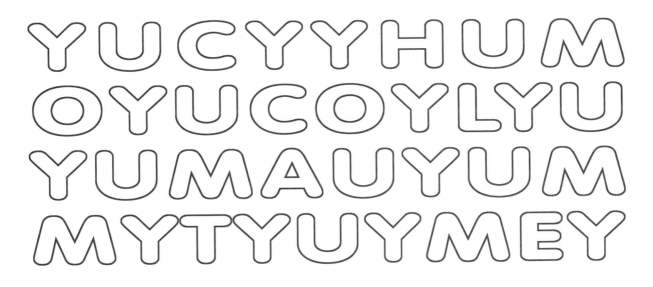

Half a Bar Is Better Than None!

Greg has found half of a "**KACKLE**" bar in his goodie bag. Can you find the other half?

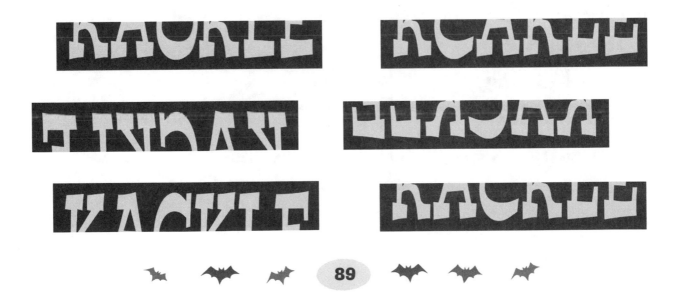

Larry's List

Larry likes a lot of different candies, but his favorite one is hidden in this list. Can you figure out what it is?

gumdropS
licOrice
chewing gUm
candy coRn
chocolate
BArs
loLLipops
peppermintS

- - - - - - - - - - - - - - - - - - -

Sandy's Candies

Sandy had a trick-or-treat bag with candies in it. Can you tell how many candies were in her bag using this clue?

Sandy took no candies from her bag, and she left no candies in her bag.

START

Candy Corn

Find your way from START to END.
EXTRA: Which one candy corn has backwards colors?

END

Mystery Treats

Someone forgot to put names on these recipe cards. Can you tell from the ingredients what they were making from each one? Write the name of the finished food at the top of each card.

Recipe 1: _____

1 1/2 Tbsp. butter
1 1/2 cups corn syrup
6 Tbsp. water
6 cups popped corn

Recipe 2: _____

1 cup water
2 cups sugar
1 cup corn syrup
1 tsp. salt

3 Tbsp. butter
1/2 tsp. baking soda
1 tsp. vanilla
2 cups shelled peanuts

Recipe 3: _____

1/2 cup butter
4 cups mini-marshmallows
6 cups crisped rice cereal

Recipe 4: _____

1 package caramel candies
1/2 cup water
8 apples
8 small, flat, wooden sticks

Recipe 5: _____

3 cups semi-sweet chocolate chips
1 can sweetened condensed milk
1 cup chopped nuts (optional)
dash salt
1 1/2 tsp. vanilla

Lost My Lollipop!

Can you find the one time where the word **LOLLIPOP** is spelled correctly?

```
L O L I P O P L O
O L O L O L I O L
L O L O L O L L L
L O L I P O O L I
I L I L O L L I P
P L P O L P O L O
P O L I O L L O P
O L P O L O I O L
P O O L I O P L O
P I L L O L L I P
```

Definitely Delicious

Candy is as tasty as tasty can be! How many words can you make from the word **D-E-L-I-C-I-O-U-S**? We bet you can make at least 25. Give yourself an extra smack of the lips if you get any words of five letters or longer.

DELICIOUS

1. _____   9. _____   17. _____

2. _____   10. _____   18. _____

3. _____   11. _____   19. _____

4. _____   12. _____   20. _____

5. _____   13. _____   21. _____

6. _____   14. _____   22. _____

7. _____   15. _____   23. _____

8. _____   16. _____   24. _____

Wax___

Candy___

Root Beer___

Gummy___

Licorice___

Chocolate___

Weird, but Tasty
Candy can be fun, but funny, too! Some of our favorites come in strange shapes, with odd flavors and silly names. See if you can match the candy flavor on the left with the proper "unusual" shape on the right.

1. Worm

2. Turtle

3. Shoelaces

4. Lips

5. Barrel

6. Buttons

Who Got What?

Dotty and her twin sister went trick-or-treating at the same houses, but did they get the same candy? Find the two candies that do not appear in both bags.

That's a Whole Lot of Candy!

Halloween is the top "candy holiday" in the United States. Use the candy decoder to figure out how much money Americans spend on candy in just one year!

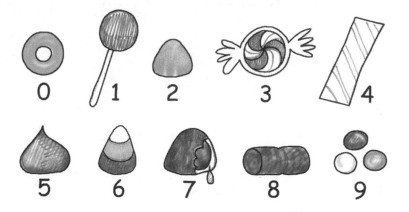

0 1 2 3 4

5 6 7 8 9

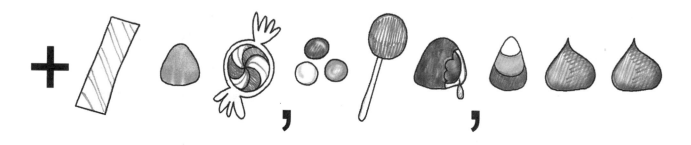

Hey, Bill, what's the difference between a baseball glove and a candy bar?

Hey, Will, if you can't tell the difference, I'll take your candy bar!

Candy Hunt

Can you find the 16 places where the word CANDY is hidden in this picture?

Candy Costume

Want to make a costume that's good enough to eat? Why not turn yourself into a goodie bag?

To make the candies:

● You will need a collection of small boxes, pieces of Styrofoam, swimming pool "noodles"—anything lightweight with an interesting shape will do.

● Wrap each item in brightly colored foil wrapping paper, and decorate with stripes of construction paper or colored duct tape, and swirls of poster paint.

● Then wrap each candy in a square of clear or colored cellophane, twisting the ends and tying them with ribbon.

To make the goodie bag:

You will need a large roll of clear cellophane, a roll of clear packing tape, and two strips of wide ribbon or fabric.

1.

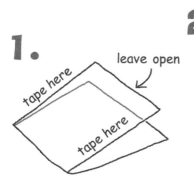

leave open

tape here

tape here

Take sheet of cellophane and fold in half. Tape both sides closed with clear tape. Leave top open to form a pocket. Make two!

2.

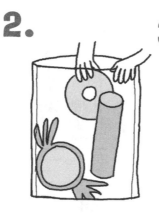

Stuff pockets with "candies."

3.

Seal tops of pockets with clear tape. Use tape to attach two straps.

4.

One goodie bag goes in front, and one in back. You're in the middle!

In the Dark!

You will need a gel pen or a light colored pencil. Starting at number 1, connect the dots to see how this traditional tale ends. When you're done with the numbered dots, take a dime and place it on each of the three dots without a number. Trace around the dime to complete the picture.

In a dark, dark house was a dark, dark room. In the dark, dark room was a dark, dark cupboard. In the dark, dark cupboard was a dark, dark shelf. On the dark, dark shelf was a dark, dark box. And in the dark, dark box was a dark, dark . . .

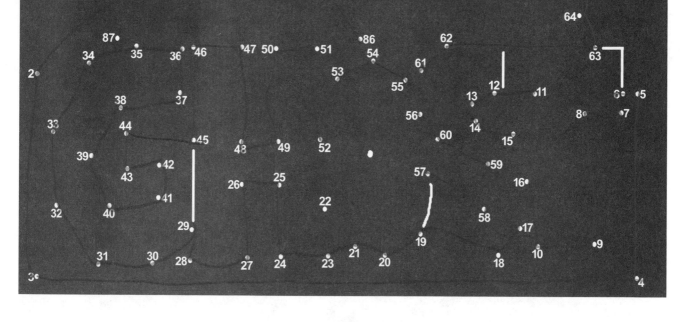

No Sleep Sleepover

Kids love to tell scary stories. Can you spy where each of these small parts is located in the big picture? Shade in the ones you find. **HINT:** The small parts might be turned sideways or upside down.

Goodness Gracious!

We found this strange writing on our computer screen this morning. We think it might be the start of a scary story. Can you crack the keyboard code and figure out what it says?

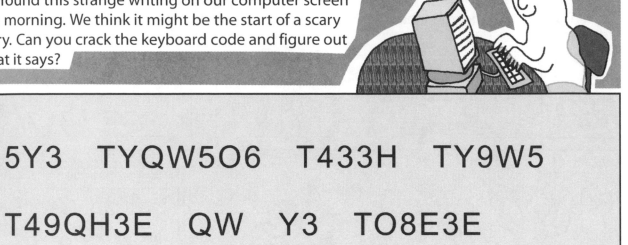

5Y3 TYQW5O6 T433H TY9W5

T49QH3E QW Y3 TO8E3E

T48JO6 Q497HE Y8W T73W5W.

5Y3 T4970 TQW03E, QHE Y3

2QW T9H3. T99EG63!

Scary Synonyms

Synonyms are words that have the same, or almost the same, meaning. We have chosen four synonyms for each word listed below. How quickly can you find them in the word list and write them where they belong? Can you fit all the ones that start with the letter "S" into the crisscross?
HINT: You don't have to put **S-C-R-E-A-M** into the grid—it's already there to help you out!

SCREAM = _____ _____ _____ _____

DARK = _____ _____ _____ _____

SMASH = _____ _____ _____ _____

DAMP = _____ _____ _____ _____

SCARE = _____ _____ _____ _____

DANGEROUS = _____ _____ _____ _____

ALARM   BREAK
CLAMMY   CRUMBLE
CRUSH   DEMOLISH
DIM   FRIGHTEN
GLOOMY   HAZARDOUS
HOWL   MOIST
MURKY   PERILOUS
RISKY   SHOCK
SHOUT   SHRIEK
SOGGY   STARTLE
SUNLESS   UNSAFE
WET   YELL

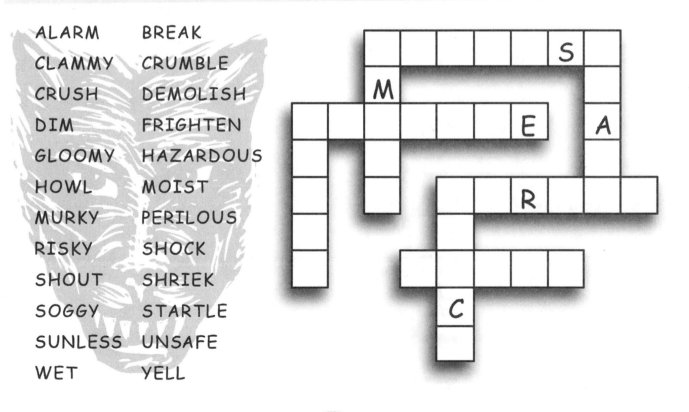

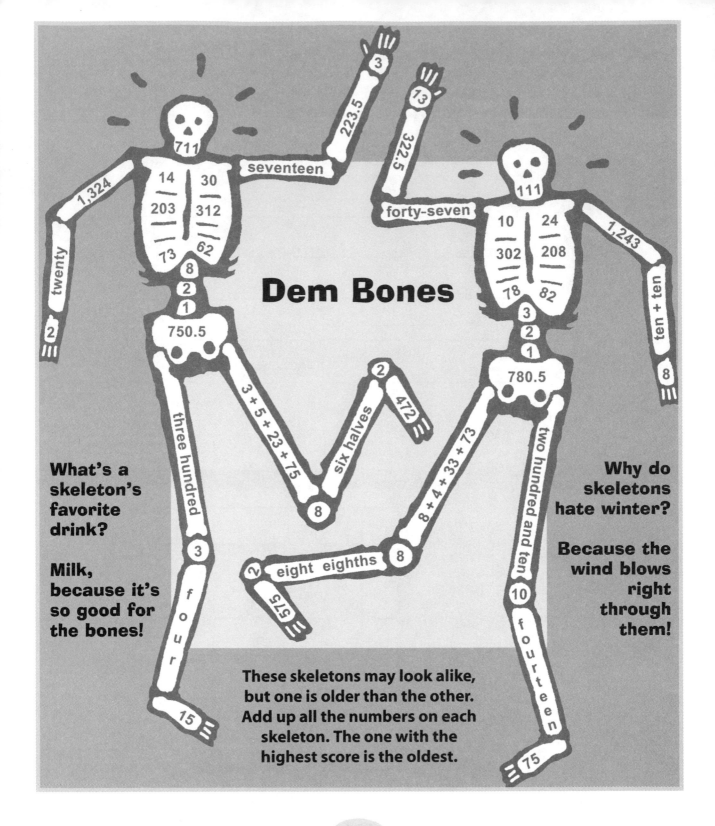

Dem Bones

What's a skeleton's favorite drink?

Milk, because it's so good for the bones!

Why do skeletons hate winter?

Because the wind blows right through them!

These skeletons may look alike, but one is older than the other. Add up all the numbers on each skeleton. The one with the highest score is the oldest.

Famous Last Words

There is a folktale about a man whose bride always wears a ribbon around her neck. He wants her to take it off, but she never will. One day he removes it—and her head falls off! Solve this puzzle to see what were her last words to him.

Answer as many clues as you can and fill them into the grid. Work back and forth between the box and the clues until you have both completed.

A. A hammer or saw

T̲ O̲ O̲ L̲
2   10 15 14

B. A small, round mark

_̲_ _̲_ _̲_
14   7   16

C. A small shelter

_̲_ _̲_ _̲_
17   8   19

D. Opposite of "out of"

_̲_ _̲_ _̲_ _̲_
1   9   12   3

E. Day between yesterday and tomorrow

_̲_ _̲_ _̲_ _̲_ _̲_
11 13   5   18   6

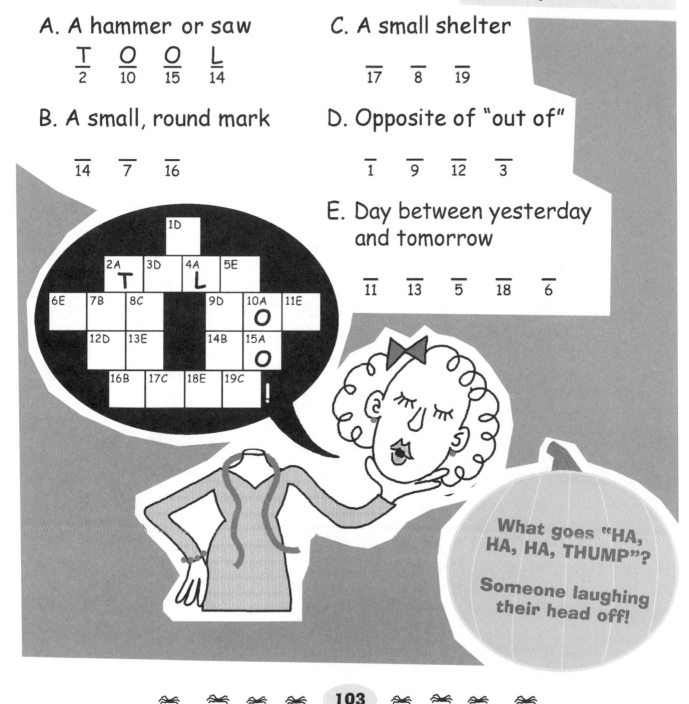

What goes "HA, HA, HA, THUMP"?

Someone laughing their head off!

Home Alone

Ask a friend or someone in your family to help create this scary story. Don't show them the story first! Just ask them for the kind of word you need for each blank spot (a description is written underneath). Write the words your helper gives you in the blanks, then read the story out loud. Don't be surprised if the story is more silly than scary! **HINT:** Use pencil so you can do it again with different words.

_____ was home alone. It was dark. It was quiet.
family member's name

Suddenly, _____ heard a _____ _____.
same name   adjective   sound

What could it be? _____ _____ down the
same name   action, past tense

stairs. In the _____ was _____. He was
room in house   boy's name

holding a _____. His _____ was bleeding. His
thing   body part

_____ was black and _____, and swollen to the size
different body part   color

of a _____. "_____! What happened ?" cried
big thing   sound of surprise

_____. As _____ _____
same family member's name   same boy's name   action, past tense

to the floor, he gasped, "Beware the _____ _____
adjective   pattern

_____!"
Halloween creature

Heads Up!

Ride from **START** to **I'M OVER HERE!** to help the legendary headless horseman find his head.

START

Enormous Autographs

Four famous authors of creepy stories have signed their books, but they wrote their names too big! Part of each first name is on the top line and part of each second name is on the bottom line. Using the list provided, can you figure out which author has signed which book?

Bram Stoker
R. L. Stine

Gaston Leroux
Washington Irving

Edgar Allan Poe
J. K. Rowling

Mary Shelley
Stephen King

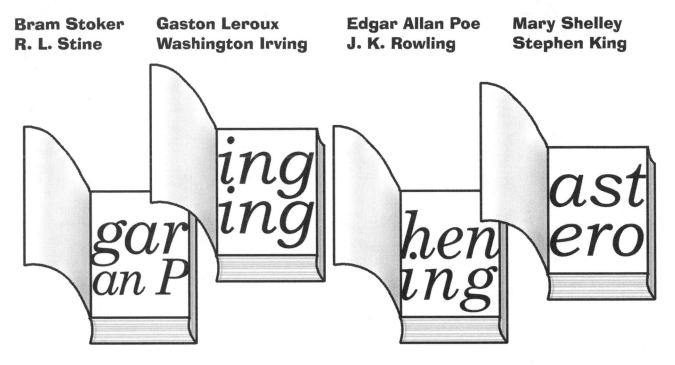

Telltale Title

This classic horror story has been in the library so long that the book title has partly worn off. Can you figure out the title and the author? **HINT:** This story features the legendary headless horseman.

Super Spooky Word

Many scary stories have ghostly visions, creatures who change shape, and mysterious things that happen for no reason. Here is a long word that is commonly used to describe these kinds of uncommon events. Place a letter in each space to make a three-letter word reading from top to bottom. When you have done it correctly, you will find the super spooky word reading from left to right across the shaded boxes!

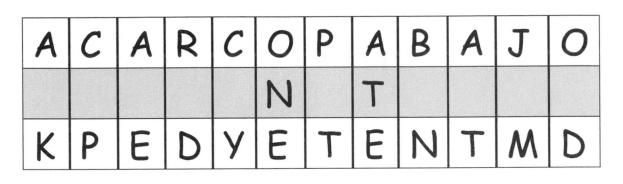

A	C	A	R	C	O	P	A	B	A	J	O
					N		T				
K	P	E	D	Y	E	T	E	N	T	M	D

Story Starter

The popular first line for a spooky story is hidden in the words below. To find it, cross out the following kinds of words, and read the leftover words from left to right, and top to bottom.

- Words that start with the letter O
- Words with double letters
- Words that rhyme with "scary"
- Creatures with pointy teeth

OVER	WOLF	BOOK	IT	SCATTER
RAT	WAS	HAIRY	ONCE	A
YELLOW	SNAKE	DARK	CAT	WARY
AND	ON	ROOM	OPEN	STORMY
FAIRY	BROOM	NIGHT	LITTLE	BAT

Creepy Compounds

Using the picture clues, figure out these four compound words that are often used in scary stories.

EXTRA FUN: Can you use these four words when telling the story, below?

Spooked

Look at the six pictures below. Can you number them correctly so that the story makes sense?

Appendix A
Halloween Web Sites

There are oodles of fun Halloween Web sites to visit. Here are a few of our favorites.

✑ www.yahooligans.com

When you get to the home page of this site, type "HALLOWEEN" in the search box that's in the center of the page. Hit ENTER, and you'll get a list that includes: how to send Halloween e-cards and messages, "Ask Earl" about the history of Halloween, Halloween news, and current info in the "Big Picture." You'll also find costume ideas, recipes, safety tips, pumpkin carving patterns, and clip art! Plus, there is a handy link to put you in touch with the UNICEF organization to find out how to get your own coin collecting box for this year's trick-or-treating.

✑ www.BlackDog.net/holiday/halloween

The Black Dog site always has fun stuff, so you won't be surprised at the great collection of activities, games, music, and ideas that will help you get in the mood for Halloween.

✑ www.benjerry.com/halloween

These ice cream experts offer cool and creepy Halloween fun! Check out the flavor graveyard, haunted house, desktop wallpaper, games, coloring pages, crafts, history, and more!

✑ www.trickortreats.com

This site is sponsored by Hershey's candy. It offers ghostly treats, ghoulish games, creepy free stuff, spooky activities, as well as resources for teachers and parents. You will be familiar with many of the candies that are used in the craft projects!

✑ www.halloweenkids.com

Enjoy coloring, games, and celebrations around the world! Get ideas on how to host a UNICEF party, create a costume, or decorate a pumpkin.

✑ www.night.net/halloween/halloween-carols.html-ssi

You need to be careful typing in this Web address, but it's worth it. Lots of your favorite songs and carols have been rewritten with Halloween words. The music is so great, you will definitely want to sing along. Fun graphics, too!

Appendix B

Halloween "Do" List

Here is a list of things you can do to make your Halloween as safe as it is fun:

1. **DO** trick-or-treat with a friend.

2. **DO** stay in your own neighborhood.

3. **DO** go only to houses with their lights on.

4. **DO** use sidewalks and driveways.

5. **DO** cross streets at the corner or in a crosswalk.

6. **DO** walk (rather than run).

7. **DO** wear a flame-retardant costume.

8. **DO** carry a flashlight.

9. **DO** be cautious of strangers.

10. **DO** say thank you.

11. **DO** check candy before eating it.

12. **DO** wear a watch and get home on time.

13. **DO** have fun!

Puzzle Answers

page v • Introduction

L N R O M A G E
P R E T A C O G
P O T A T O E S
A C T P H I G E
B O U R U N G L
E R B E E S S A

page 2 • Tasty Pastry

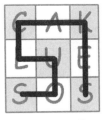

SOUL CAKES

page 2 • Seeing the Future

THE FIRST INITIAL
OF THEIR SWEETHEART

page 3 • Why a Disguise?

1K	2G	3D	4K		5H	6D	7I	8E	9C		10C	11B			
T	H	E	Y		H	O	P	E	D		I	T			
12J	13K	14I	15I	16F		17A	18F	19G	20E		21A	22D	23A	24E	
W	O	U	L	D		K	E	E	P		E	V	I	L	
25B	26H	27F	28D	29J	30A	31G		32B	33F	34H	35I				
S	P	I	R	I	T	S		A	W	A	Y				
36B	37H	38G	39C		40J	41E	42C	43I							
F	R	O	M		T	H	E	M							

A. Toy that is flown at the end of a long string.

$\underset{17}{K}\ \underset{23}{I}\ \underset{30}{T}\ \underset{21}{E}$

B. Opposite of slow.

$\underset{36}{F}\ \underset{32}{A}\ \underset{25}{S}\ \underset{11}{T}$

C. Ten cents.

$\underset{9}{D}\ \underset{10}{I}\ \underset{39}{M}\ \underset{42}{E}$

D. Opposite of under.

$\underset{6}{O}\ \underset{22}{V}\ \underset{3}{E}\ \underset{28}{R}$

E. Give someone a hand.

$\underset{41}{H}\ \underset{8}{E}\ \underset{24}{L}\ \underset{20}{P}$

F. Opposite of narrow.

$\underset{33}{W}\ \underset{27}{I}\ \underset{16}{D}\ \underset{18}{E}$

G. What you wear on a foot.

$\underset{31}{S}\ \underset{2}{H}\ \underset{38}{O}\ \underset{19}{E}$

H. Musical instrument with strings.

$\underset{5}{H}\ \underset{34}{A}\ \underset{37}{R}\ \underset{26}{P}$

I. Mashed potatoes should not be this way.

$\underset{15}{L}\ \underset{14}{U}\ \underset{43}{M}\ \underset{7}{P}\ \underset{35}{Y}$

J. Ability to make clever jokes.

$\underset{12}{W}\ \underset{29}{I}\ \underset{40}{T}$

K. Something to play with.

$\underset{1}{T}\ \underset{13}{O}\ \underset{4}{Y}$

Puzzle Answers

page 4 • Orange and Black

Orange fruits for carving.
P U M P K I N S

A golden summer flower.
M A R I G O L D

Gather ripe crops.
H A R V E S T

They turn orange in autumn.
L E A V E S

Flickering tongues of fire.
F L A M E S

A bright light in the sky at night.
M O O N

You write on it with chalk.
B L A C K B O A R D

Furry pets that catch mice.
C A T S

Sidewalk or street covering.
P A V E M E N T

Opposite of day.
N I G H T

Opposite of life.
D E A T H

A web-spinner.
S P I D E R

What does "orange" represent?
LIGHTNESS

What does "black" represent?
DARKNESS

page 6 • How Symbolic

page 5 • You Look Familiar

page 5 • Celtic Celebration

~~CHRISTMAS~~
S ~~FASSIKA~~ A
~~PURIMHOLI~~
M ~~CARNIVAL~~
~~KWANZAAHA~~
I N ~~NEWYEAR~~

S A M H A I N

112

Puzzle Answers

page 7 • Superstitious Words

Some possible answers:

in	is	it	net	no	nose	not	notes
on	one	person	pert	pest	pier	piston	pit
pore	port	ports	pose	press	prone	prose	pun
pure	purse	puss	put	rent	rest	rip	ripe
rise	rope	rose	sent	sip	sit	so	son
spin	spine	spit	spore	sport	sports	spot	spurt
stone	strip	stripe	stripes	sun	super	sure	ten
tent	tie	tin	tip	tires	to	ton	tone
tore	up	use					

page 8 • Day of the Dead

1. Passed on
2. Deceased
3. Lifeless
4. Perished
5. Departed

page 9 • Double Trouble

Answer 1:
"Double, double, toil and trouble
Fire burn, and cauldron bubble."
Answer 2:
Salem, Mass.

page 8 • Bread of the Dead

page 10 • Creepy Carving

Puzzle Answers

page 11 • Hello Again

```
    H O O P
  B A L L S
    R O P E
S W O R D
L A D Y
```

```
    H A T
  C O I N S
    C U P S
C A R D S
R A B B I T
    W A N D
S T R I N G
```

page 14 • Yummy Pumpkins

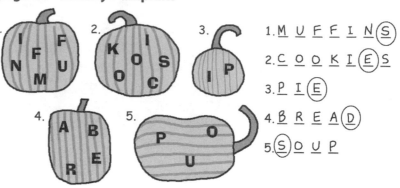

1. M U F F I N S
2. C O O K I E S
3. P I E
4. B R E A D
5. S O U P

page14 • Smashed Pumpkins

page 12 • Burning Bonfire

page 15 • Carve-a-thon

1. DAS   SAD
2. DSPRSURIE   SURPRISED
3. NIKIWNG   WINKING
4. YFOOG   GOOFY
5. RASCY   SCARY
6. YOTOTH   TOOTHY

page 15 • Pumpkin Patch

114

Puzzle Answers

page 16 • Smile!

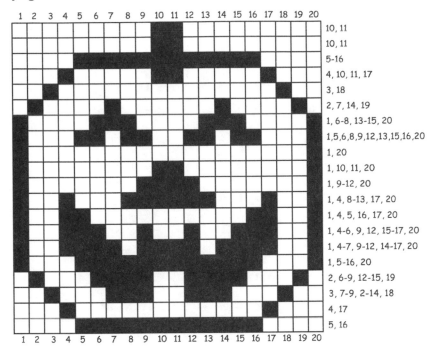

10, 11
10, 11
5-16
4, 10, 11, 17
3, 18
2, 7, 14, 19
1, 6-8, 13-15, 20
1,5,6,8,9,12,13,15,16,20
1, 20
1, 10, 11, 20
1, 9-12, 20
1, 4, 8-13, 17, 20
1, 4, 5, 16, 17, 20
1, 4-6, 9, 12, 15-17, 20
1, 4-7, 9-12, 14-17, 20
1, 5-16, 20
2, 6-9, 12-15, 19
3, 7-9, 2-14, 18
4, 17
5, 16

page 17 •How Big?

THE WORLD'S LARGEST
PUMPKINS CAN GROW TO
BE OVER ONE THOUSAND
POUNDS. AWESOME!

page 17 • Sad Jack / Glad Jack

page 18 • Squiggle Giggles

Finished drawings will all be very
different from each other!

page 19 • Wacky Word

A "plumpkin"!

115

Puzzle Answers

page 19 • Missing Pumpkin

A color	P U R P L E
A room in your house	K I T C H E N
Played on instruments	M U S I C
Covers you while you sleep	B L A N K E T
Go out of sight	D I S A P P E A R
Eat this at the movies	P O P C O R N
To talk	S P E A K
Apples or oranges	F R U I T
Goes on a letter	S T A M P
Part of your finger	K N U C K L E

page 20 • Pumpkin Rings

S C A R Y F A C E S W E R E
C A R V E D I N T O
T U R N I P S, B E E T S,
O R P O T A T O E S.

page 21 • Pounds of Pumpkins

Some possible answers are listed below. If you have a different solution, but it equals the amount shown, you've got a right answer!

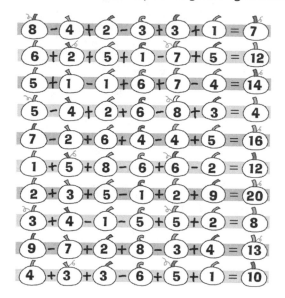

8 − 4 + 2 − 3 + 3 + 1 = 7
6 + 2 + 5 + 1 − 7 + 5 = 12
5 + 1 − 1 + 6 + 7 − 4 = 14
5 − 4 + 2 + 6 − 8 + 3 = 4
7 − 2 + 6 + 4 − 4 + 5 = 16
1 + 5 + 8 − 6 + 6 − 2 = 12
2 + 3 + 5 − 1 + 2 + 9 = 20
3 + 4 − 1 − 5 + 5 + 2 = 8
9 − 7 + 2 + 8 − 3 + 4 = 13
4 + 3 + 3 − 6 + 5 + 1 = 10

page 22 • Perfect Pumpkin

Puzzle Answers

page 23 • Copy Cat

1. The two crows are facing in opposite directions.
2. One hat has a flower, one doesn't.
3. Mouths have different number of teeth on top.
4. Sticks that poke out from behind the right shoulders are different lengths.
5. Right button on overall straps are different shapes.
6. One shirt has patch on right shoulder, one doesn't.
7. "Mike" spelled wrong on one pocket.
8. Button on right shirt cuff is in a different position.
9. Thumb on left hand is either in front of, or behind, the leg.
10. Right hand has different number of fingers.
11. Small patch on right leg in different position.
12. Big patch on left leg has different number of stitches.
13. Sock on left foot is missing the stitches on the toe.

page 24 • Rebus Riddle
A "life gourd" (lifeguard)!

page 24 • Piece of Pie

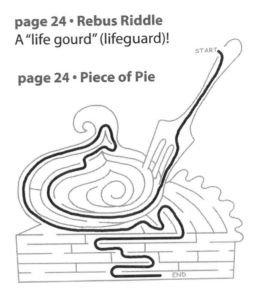

page 26 • Creepy Crisscross

KEE	EEK
OBO	BOO
OLHW	HOWL
OTOH	HOOT
UHDT	THUD
AONM	MOAN
NLAKC	CLANK
ORAGN	GROAN
WOLRG	GROWL
CLAKCE	CACKLE
ARCESM	SCREAM
QELUSA	SQUEAL
LTRAET	RATTLE

page 26 • Spider Speak

ANSWER:
How do you boo?

Puzzle Answers

page 27 • Haunted Hink Pinks

What does a spook have for breakfast?

G H O S T   T O A S T

What did the witch use to clean the cemetery?

T O M B   B R O O M

What is a fast prank?

Q U I C K   T R I C K

What is a wealthy woman who casts spells?

R I C H   W I T C H

What is a scary evening?

F R I G H T   N I G H T

What is a really good bunch of magic words?

S W E L L   S P E L L

What is a small, really thin, furry animal that flies?

F L A T   B A T

BONUS: What is a fun Halloween gathering for kids all dressed as Albert Einstein?

S M A R T Y   P A R T Y

page 27 • Ghostly Message

Answer:
Hide and Shriek

page 28 • Any Body Home?

page 29 • Time for Tea

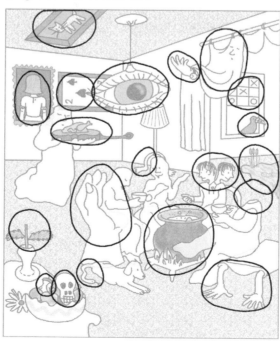

page 30 • Haunted Words

Possible answers:

and	hut
ant	net
at	neat
ate	due
aunt	nut
date	tan
death	tea
den	ten
dent	tend
eat	than
had	the
hat	then
hate	thud
he	tuna
head	tune
heat	tuned
hunt	

page 30 • Which Window?

Puzzle Answers

page 31 • Going Batty

page 31 • Just Like a Vampire

page 32 • Spider's Choice
French flies!

page 32 • Creaking Stairs

PEAK
top of a mountain

LEAK
to drip through a hole

WEAK
not having strength or power

SNEAK
to move secretly and quietly

CREAK
a sharp, squeaking sound

FREAK
anything odd or unusual

BLEAK
cold and gloomy

SPEAK
to talk or use words

STREAK
a long, thin mark

page 33 • Giggly Gravestones

119

Puzzle Answers

page 34 • Boo Who?

page 35 • What's So Funny?
To speak "spooktalk," you add the letters BOO after *every* letter in a word! When you cross out all the BOOs, the riddle reads:

What is a ghost's favorite snack food? Donut holes!

page 35 • Who's Haunting the House?
When you look at the empty door or window of the house after staring at the black face, you will see the "afterimage" of the face glowing and flickering.

page 36 • It's a Spooky Day in the Neighborhood

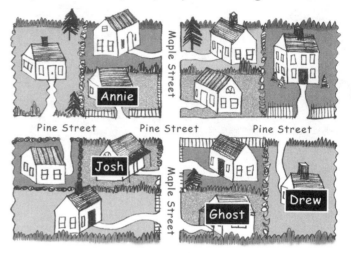

page 38 • The Big Picture

Puzzle Answers

page 40 • Movin' On

START

GRAVE	YARD	WORK	HORSE
STONE	STICK	HAND	BALL
WALL	PAPER	BACK	YARD
BACK	CLIP	HAND	RAIL
BONE	WHITE	BACK	ROAD

END

page 40 • Just Joking!

What would you name a monster with no arms and no legs who is . . .

. . . floating in a pool? BOB

. . . hanging on a wall? ART

. . . lying by a door? MATT

page 41 • Fright Night

page 42 • Grandmonster

1) How often do next women clean? $10 + 1 + 2 = 13$

2) It won't snow into next week. $2 + 1 = 3$

3) The freight train won't enter the station until six o'clock. $8 + 10 + 6 = 24$

4) Pat won three gymnastic medals even after falling down. $2 + 3 + 7 = 12$

5) Seth reeked after camping for two weeks. $3 + 2 = 5$

6) I'm sorry if I've gone away for too long. $5 + 1 = 6$

7) Kate needs to lose weight. $10 + 8 = 18$

8) If our cat won't be careful, he will lose one of his nine lives. $4 + 2 + 1 + 9 = 16$

TOTAL:
$13 + 3 + 24 + 12 + 5 + 6 + 18 + 16 = 97$

page 43 • Monster Mama

A.   B.   C.

B.   C.   A.

page 43 • Where's My Mummy?

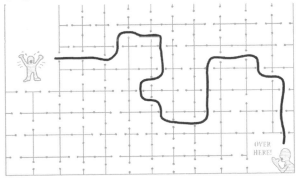

OVER HERE!

Puzzle Answers

page 44 • Extra, Extra

Where does a lady monster keep her spare parts?

1F **S**	2F **H**	3B **E**		4A **K**	5C **E**	6F **E**	7A **P**	8F **S**
9E **T**	10B **H**	11A **E**	12D **M**		13E **I**	14B **N**		15E **H**	16A **E**	17C **R**
18D **H**	19C **A**	20E **N**	21F **D**	22C **B**	23D **A**	24C **G**		

A. To continue to have.
<u>K</u> <u>E</u> <u>E</u> <u>P</u>
 4 11 16 7

B. A female chicken.
<u>H</u> <u>E</u> <u>N</u>
10 3 14

C. A boat with a flat bottom.
<u>B</u> <u>A</u> <u>R</u> <u>G</u> <u>E</u>
22 19 17 24 5

D. Meat from a pig.
<u>H</u> <u>A</u> <u>M</u>
18 23 12

E. Opposite of fat.
<u>T</u> <u>H</u> <u>I</u> <u>N</u>
 9 15 13 20

F. Small storage buildings.
<u>S</u> <u>H</u> <u>E</u> <u>D</u> <u>S</u>
 8 2 6 21 1

page 46 • Double Up

page 48 • Monster Merge

... a monster and a cow?
A "<u>M O O S T E R</u>"

... a mad scientist and a famous piano?
A "<u>F R A N K E N S T E I N W A Y</u>"

... a monster and a lot of money?
A "<u>G O D Z I L L I O N</u>"

... junk food and a vampire?
"<u>S N A C K U L A</u>"

... a vampire and a soda?
"<u>D R A C O L A</u>"

... a male witch and an anteater?
A "<u>W I Z A A R D V A R K</u>"

page 50 • Bits and Pieces

1. witch
2. bumblebee
3. scarecrow
4. cat (or mouse!)
5. clown
6. dalmatian dog
7. skeleton
8. vampire
9. sheriff (or cowboy)

page 50 • Family Fun

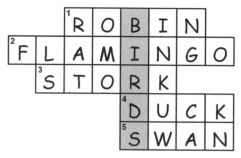

122

Puzzle Answers

page 51 • What's That You Say?

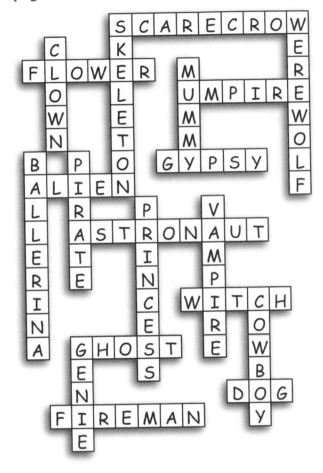

page 53 • Quick Change
Here is one possible answer.

SHEET

GHEET

GHOET

GHOST

page 54 • Mirror, Mirror

SOME KIDS
WILL LIKE
CHRISTA'S
COSTUME,
AND SOME
WILL NOT!

page 52 • Dress Him Up

Answers:
1) bandana
2) parrot
3) hook
4) earring
5) patch
6) moustache
7) boots
8) scar
9) sword
10) hair

Everybody's pirate drawing will look a little different. Here's ours!

page 55 • What to Wear?

BONUS:
ONE AND A HALF BILLION DOLLARS IS SPENT

123

Puzzle Answers

page 56 • Costly Costumes

WITCH

Pointy hat	$2.95
Black gown	$4.50
Cauldron	$3.75
Broom	$2.50
Wart	$ .50
Bat	$1.25
Ugly nose	$1.00
Face paint kit	$2.00
Wig	$1.75
	$20.20

CLOWN

Wig	$3.50
Face paint kit	$2.00
Squirt flower	$1.25
Big bowtie	$2.50
Floppy shoes	$3.75
Funny hat	$2.25
Floppy costume	$3.00
Bulb nose	$ .50
	$18.75

BALLERINA

Tutu	$4.95
Ballet slippers	$3.50
Crown	$2.95
Lip gloss	$ .75
Tights	$1.75
	$13.90

COWGIRL

Hat	$3.95
Vest	$2.50
Hobby horse	$2.75
Boots	$4.25
Holster	$1.95
Bandana	$ .75
Rope	$1.50
	$17.65

Annie can easily afford to be a ballerina. If she wants to be something else, she'll have to buy less stuff!

page 58 • Many Masks

page 59 • All Wrapped Up!

page 59 • Mumbling Mummy

Sticky and chewy.
<u>G</u> UMMY

Another word for stomach.
<u>T</u> UMMY

Not very good.
<u>C R</u> UMMY

Delicious!
<u>Y</u> UMMY

page 60 • What's Dot?   A butterfly!

124

Puzzle Answers

page 62 • Perfect Timing

ETHAN   KELLY   ALIEN   PETER   OLIVIA

page 62 • Taking Treats
Ethan took four treats, Peter and Olivia each took three treats, the real alien took four treats, and Kelly took one treat.

page 63 • Looking for Letters
"Trick-or-Treat, smell my feet, give me something good to eat."

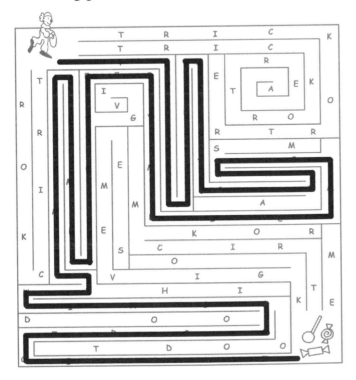

page 64 • Short Cut

page 65 • House to House

HOUSE	WORK	PLACE	MAT	OPEN
BOAT	HOUSE	FLY	AWAY	SKY
BACK	HOLD	PAPER	WEIGHT	LESS
ACHE	UP	BACK	YARD	STICK
COOL	WIND	FIRE	WOOD	STOVE
DOWN	FALL	SIDE	WIND	FALL
POUR	SLOW	PITCH	BLACK	OUT
HAND	BOOK	CASE	LOAD	HOUSE

page 65 • Under Wraps
Throw away any unwrapped candy.

Puzzle Answers

page 66 • Trick or Treat?
Trick Answer

Treat Answer

page 67 • Coin-Incidentally

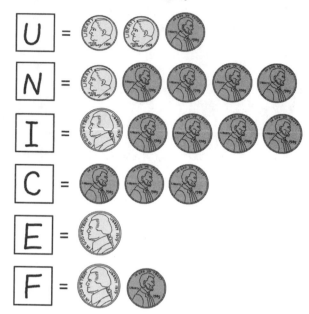

page 68 • Lights Out!
Remaining luminaries are 1, 2, 2, and 3. Added = 8

page 68 • Witch Walk
She was hoping for a charm bracelet.

page 69 • Safety Matters

TULDA = adult	THIGSHLAFL = flashlight
THIGLS = lights	FLEMA = flame
LAWK = walk	GRNATSRES = strangers
OYU ANKTH = thank you	REVEN = never
GINTEA = eating	BROODHOGONEI = neighborhood

1. Young children should always trick-or-treat with an <u>ADULT</u>.
2. <u>NEVER</u> trick-or-treat by yourself.
3. Wear a <u>FLAME</u>-retardant costume.
4. Check candy before <u>EATING</u> it.
5. Only visit houses with the <u>LIGHTS</u> on.
6. Carry a <u>FLASHLIGHT</u> at night.
7. Don't forget to say "<u>THANK YOU</u>."

Puzzle Answers

page 70 • Scared Skeleton

A. Nickname for Theodore
T E D
8 15 3

D. Item worn on the head
H A T
9 10 18

B. Home for a bee
H I V E
1 4 11 2

E. Spirit of a dead person
G H O S T
16 14 7 19 13

C. A large mound of sand
D U N E
5 17 6 12

Crossword answer:
HE
DID
NOT
HAVE
THE
GUTS!

page 71 • Sorting the Loot

- HOW MANY DIFFERENT KINDS OF TREATS ARE THERE? There are 12 different kinds: gum, sticker, chocolate "coco" bar, lollipop, YUM YUM YUM candy, coin, candy corn (each bagful counts as one), swirly mints, spider ring, chocolate chip cookie, Bitz candy, fireball.

- OF WHICH TREAT IS THERE ONLY ONE? There is only one fireball.

- WHICH TREAT WAS GIVEN THE MOST? Lollipops (there are 11), though chocolate is a close second with 10 pieces.

- HOW MUCH DO THE COINS ADD UP TO? $2.50

- WHICH IS YOUR FAVORITE TREAT? Everyone will have a different favorite!

- ARE THERE MORE SPIDER RINGS OR SWIRLY MINTS? There are the same number (8).

page 72 • Windy Night

page 74 • Where's the Party?

The invitation was sent by a werewolf. It reads:

Have a howling good time at a Halloween party Friday, October 31 6:00 – 9:00 pm Come in costume to Ima Wolfe's house, 13 Spooky Trail Snarlsville, NY RSVP 313-1313

THIRD
HOUSE
ON THE
LEFT

page 75 • Donut on a String

CHOCOLATE, POWDERED, GLAZED, SPRINKLED, COCONUT.

Puzzle Answers

page 75 • Bobbing for Apples

BO**BB**IN   a spool for winding thread
BO**BC**AT   a small wildcat
BO**BS**LED   a long sled for racing
BO**BW**HITE   a bird that makes a sound like its name
BO**BB**IE   a nickname for a girl named Roberta

page 76 • Perfect Plans

p<u>a</u>per <u>c</u>ups str<u>i</u>ng
apples don<u>u</u>ts
<u>c</u>ider nap<u>k</u>ins
<u>b</u>a<u>ll</u>ons p<u>o</u>p<u>c</u>o<u>r</u>n

page 77 • Ooey Gooey

EYEBALLS = peeled G R A P E S

NOSE = piece of H O T D O G

TEETH = C A N D Y C O R N

HAIR = fresh S P R O U T S

BRAIN = cooked C A U L I F L O W E R

BONES = broken B R A N C H E S

FINGERNAILS = N U T S H E L L S

FINGER = old, limp C A R R O T

GUTS = cooked, oiled S P A G H E T T I

HEART = peeled T O M A T O

page 78 • Name the Game

The name of the game is "BOOMERANG"!

Puzzle Answers

page 80 • Solitaire Hangman
Costumes: gypsy, fairy, clown, robot
Party foods: chips, candy, donut
Party favors: fangs, cards, wands

page 81 • Beanbag Toss

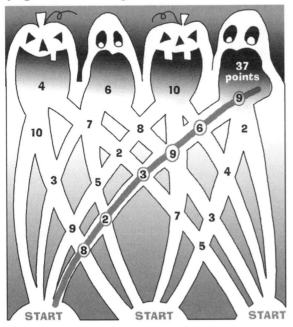

page 82 • Hide and Seek

page 83 • Ghost Bowling
Debbie: 5 pins knocked over (#1, 2, 4, 6, 7) = 20 points
Josh: 6 pins knocked over (#1, 2, 3, 5, 8, 10) = 29 points
Maxine: 4 pins knocked over (#2, 6, 9, 10) = 27 points
Josh is the winner!

EXTRA: On their second turn, figure that each player will knock over the two pins with the highest points.

Debbie: Her highest possible score would be 39.
Josh: His highest possible score would be 45.
Maxine: Her highest possible score would be 42.
Josh would still be the winner!

page 84 • Face Painting

▶ Color all numbered boxes from LEFT to RIGHT across the grid.

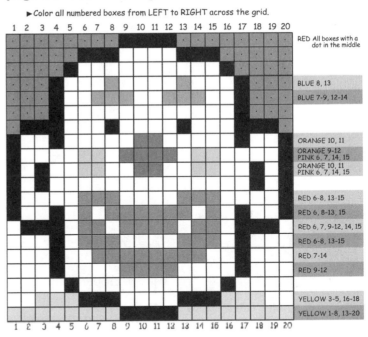

Puzzle Answers

page 86 • Where in the World?

1Q C	2I H	3Q O	4O C	5L O	6O L	7G A	8N T	9C E		10M C	11L O	12I M	13G E	14F S
15L F	16C R	17B O	18R M		19J C	20K O	21G C	22K O	23M A		24Q B	25R E	26O A	27P N	28N S
	29D T	30D H	31H A	32H T		33N A	34F R	35M E		36E G	37K R	38B O	39O W	40C N
41A O	42N N		43H C	44J A	45B C	46E A	47E O		48I T	49G R	50A E	51C E	52M S
53N I	54H N		55K T	56F H	57F E		58A T	59E R	60A O	61E P	62E I	63B C	64G A	65E L
66A R	67J E	68C G	69P I	70B O	71B N	72A S		73F O	74J F		75G T	76H H	77M E
78D W	79I O	80A R	81E L	82L D

CHOCOLATE COMES FROM COCOA BEANS THAT ARE GROWN ON CACAO TREES IN THE TROPICAL REGIONS OF THE WORLD

A. A male chicken.
R O O S T E R
66 60 41 72 58 50 80

B. Silky caterpillar case.
C O C O O N
63 70 45 38 17 71

C. Color of grass.
G R E E N
68 16 51 9 40

D. To melt.
T H A W
29 30 64 78

E. A large ape.
G O R I L L A
36 47 59 62 65 81 46

F. Land on the edge of the ocean.
S H O R E
14 56 73 34 57

G. Copy lines through a thin piece of paper.
T R A C E
75 49 7 21 13

H. Repeat words over and over.
C H A N T
43 76 31 54 32

I. Insect that looks like a butterfly.
M O T H
12 79 48 2

J. Front of the head.
F A C E
74 44 19 67

K. Plant part that grows underground.
R O O T
37 22 20 55

L. What you eat.
F O O D
15 11 5 82

M. To get away.
E S C A P E
35 52 10 23 61 77

N. A dirty spot on clothing.
S T A I N
28 8 33 53 42

O. Sharp curved nail on an animal.
C L A W
4 6 26 39

P. Opposite of out.
I N
69 27

Q. What's left when you eat fresh corn.
C O B
1 3 24

R. Opposite of you.
M E
18 25

page 87 • Whadja Get?

```
A M A N I C N V I R
G G U M B A L L S I
N I A H A N S A C G
U M W R A D P P A E
R L C C H Y A I R N
T O H H A C T I A S
O L V O E O R F M O
R L I C O R I C E T
Y I T O H N O U L S
A P N L D F E E S T
L O O A S T N I M N
G P A T N D G R O W
I S N E G T A F F Y
```

The leftover letters read: A man in Virginia has a gum wrapper chain that is over forty thousand feet long and growing!

page 88 • Dandy Candy

```
D A N D Y
P A N D A
H A N D S O M E
D E M A N D
S A N D Y
G R A N D S O N
W A N D E R
R A N D O M
A N D R O I D
I S L A N D
V A N D A L
B A N D A G E
L A N D L O R D
S A N D W I C H
C A N D Y
```

Puzzle Answers

page 89 • Favorite Flavor

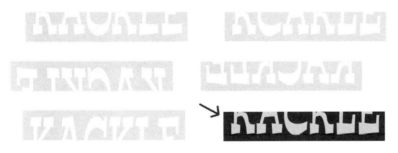

YUCYYHUM
OYUCOYLYU
YUMAUYUM
MYTYUYMEY

The answer is CHOCOLATE! (Are you surprised?)

page 89 • Half a Bar Is Better Than None!

KACKLE

page 90 • Larry's List

If you read all the capital letters in the list, you will find that Larry's favorite candy is SOURBALLS.

page 90 • Sandy's Candies

This answer is pretty tricky. There were two candies in the bag. Sandy took no cand**ies** (plural), but she took one cand**y** (singular)! Sandy left just one cand**y** in the bag, but did not leave more than one cand**ies**.

page 90 • Candy Corn

page 91 • Mystery Treats

Recipe 1: Popcorn Balls
Recipe 2: Peanut Brittle
Recipe 3: Crispy Rice Treats
Recipe 4: Caramel Apples
Recipe 5: Fudge

Puzzle Answers

page 91 • Lost My Lollipop!

```
L O L I P O P L O
O L O L O L I O L
L O L O L O L L L
L O L I P O O L I
I L I L O L L I P
P L P O L P O L O
P O L I O L L O P
O L P O L O I O L
P O O L I O P L O
P I L L O L L I P
```

page 92 • Definitely Delicious

clod	close	closed	cloud	clues	cod
code	coil	cold	dice	douse	ice
is	led	lice	lid	lied	loud
louse	old	side	sled	slice	slid
slide	sod	sold	sole	soul	us
use	used				

page 92 • Weird, but Tasty

Wax __4__

Candy __6__

Root Beer __5__

Gummy __1__

Licorice __3__

Chocolate __2__

page 93 • Who Got What?

page 94 • That's a Whole Lot of Candy!

$1,987,000,000 (one billion, 987 million dollars). Now, that's a LOT of candy!

page 95 • Candy Hunt

Puzzle Answers

page 98 • In the Dark!

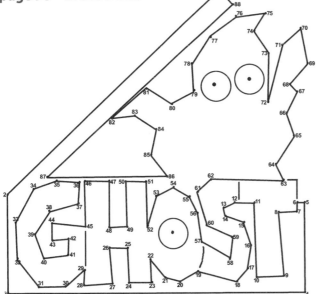

page 99 • No Sleep Sleepover

page 100 • Goodness Gracious!

The keyboard is your decoder. The correct letter is actually one row DOWN and to the RIGHT of the letter or number given. So the number 5 is actually the letter T!

THE   GHASTLY   GREEN   GHOST
5Y3   TYQW5O6   T433H   TY9W5

GROANED   AS   HE   GLIDED
T49QH3E   QW   Y3   TO8E3E

GRIMLY   AROUND   HIS   GUESTS.
T48JO6   Q497HE   Y8W   T73W5W.

THE   GROUP   GASPED,   AND   HE
5Y3   T4970   TQW03E,   QHE   Y3

WAS   GONE.   GOODBYE!
2QW   T9H3.   T99EG63!

page 101 • Scary Synonyms

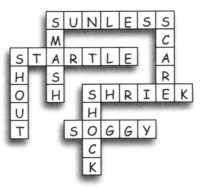

SCREAM = howl, shriek, yell, shout
DARK = dim, gloomy, sunless, murky
SMASH = break, crush, demolish, crumble
DAMP = soggy, moist, clammy, wet
SCARE = alarm, frighten, shock, startle
DANGEROUS = unsafe, risky, hazardous, perilous

page 102 • Dem Bones

The skeleton on the left has a total of 4,669. The one on the right has 4,268.

Puzzle Answers

page 103 • Famous Last Words

A. A hammer or saw
$\underline{T}_{2}$ $\underline{O}_{10}$ $\underline{O}_{15}$ $\underline{L}_{14}$

C. A small shelter
$\underline{H}_{17}$ $\underline{U}_{8}$ $\underline{T}_{19}$

B. A small, round mark
$\underline{D}_{14}$ $\underline{O}_{7}$ $\underline{T}_{16}$

D. Opposite of "out of"
$\underline{I}_{1}$ $\underline{N}_{9}$ $\underline{T}_{12}$ $\underline{O}_{3}$

E. Day between yesterday and tomorrow
$\underline{T}_{11}$ $\underline{O}_{13}$ $\underline{D}_{5}$ $\underline{A}_{18}$ $\underline{Y}_{6}$

I TOLD YOU NOT TO DO THAT!

page 104 • Home Alone

Everybody will have a totally different story! Here's ours.

Aunt Em _{family member's name} was home alone. It was dark. It was quiet.

Suddenly, Aunt Em _{same name} heard a furry _{adjective} rustle _{sound}.

What could it be? Aunt Em _{same name} swam _{action, past tense} down the

stairs. In the Kitchen _{room in house} was Ted _{boy's name}. He was

holding a boot _{thing}. His elbow _{body part} was bleeding. His

pinkie _{different body part} was black and hot pink _{color}, and swollen to the size

of a tractor trailer _{big thing}. "Eegad _{sound of surprise}! What happened ?" cried

Aunt Em _{same family member's name}. As Ted _{same boy's name} flew _{action, past tense}

to the floor, he gasped, "Beware the fluffy _{adjective} spotted _{pattern}

Vampire _{Halloween creature}!"

page 105 • Heads Up!

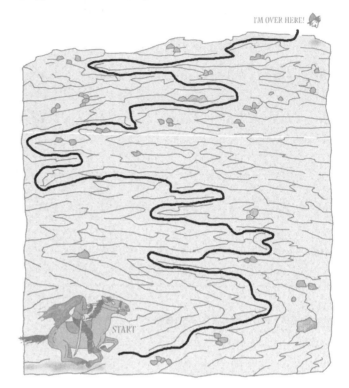

I'M OVER HERE!

START

page 106 • Enormous Autographs

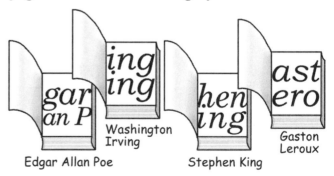

Edgar Allan Poe

Washington Irving

Stephen King

Gaston Leroux

Puzzle Answers

page 106 • Telltale Title

THE LEGEND OF SLEEPY HOLLOW by WASHINGTON IRVING

page 107 • Super Spooky Word

A	C	A	R	C	O	P	A	B	A	J	O
S	U	P	E	R	N	A	T	U	R	A	L
K	P	E	D	Y	E	T	E	N	T	M	D

page 107 • Story Starter

OVER	WOLF	BOOK	IT	SCATTER
RAT	WAS	HAIRY	ONCE	A
YELLOW	SNAKE	DARK	CAT	WARY
AND	ON	ROOM	OPEN	STORMY
FAIRY	BROOM	NIGHT	LITTLE	BAT

page 108 • Spooked

page 108 • Creepy Compounds
1. EYEBALL, 2. GRAVEYARD, 3. FOOTSTEP,
4. GOOSEBUMP

THE EVERYTHING®

KIDS'

SERIES!

Packed with tons of information, activities, and puzzles, the Everything® Kids' books are perennial bestsellers that keep kids active and engaged. Each book is 8" x 9¼", 144 pages, and two-color throughout.

All this at the incredible price of $6.95!

The Everything® Kids' Sharks Book
1-59337-304-X

The Everything® Kids' Animal
Puzzle & Activity Book
1-59337-305-8

Trade Paperback, $14.95
1-58062-147-3, 304 pages

The Everything® Bedtime Story Book

by Mark Binder

The Everything® Bedtime Story Book is a wonderfully original collection of 100 stories that will delight the entire family. Accompanied by charming illustrations, the stories included are retold in an exceptionally amusing style and are perfect for reading aloud. From familiar nursery rhymes to condensed American classics, this collection promises to promote sweet dreams, active imaginations, and quality family time.

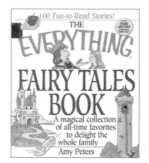

Trade Paperback, $14.95
1-58062-546-0, 304 pages

The Everything® Fairy Tales Book

by Amy Peters

Take your children to magical lands where animals talk, mythical creatures wander freely, and good and evil come in every imaginable form. You'll find all this and more in *The Everything® Fairy Tales Book*, an extensive collection of 100 classic fairy tales. This enchanting compilation features charming, original illustrations that guarantee creative imaginations and quality family time.